The Art & Craft of
Pyrography

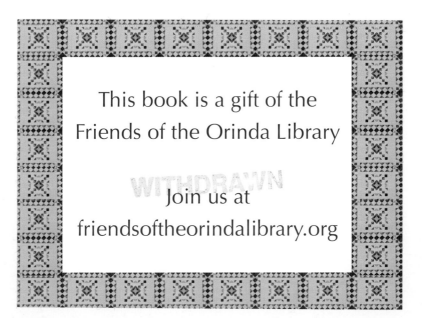

The Art & Craft of
Pyrography

Drawing with Fire on Leather, Gourds, Cloth, Paper, and Wood

Lora S. Irish

FOX CHAPEL
PUBLISHING

© 2012 by Lora S. Irish and Fox Chapel Publishing Company, Inc., East Petersburg, PA.

The Art & Craft of Pyrography is an original work, first published in 2012 by Fox Chapel Publishing Company, Inc. The projects and patterns contained herein are copyrighted by the author. Readers may make copies of these patterns for personal use. The patterns themselves, however, are not to be duplicated for resale or distribution under any circumstances. Any such copying is a violation of copyright law.

ISBN 978-1-56523-478-9

Library of Congress Cataloging-in-Publication Data

Irish, Lora S.
The art & craft of pyrography : drawing with fire on leather, gourds, cloth, paper, and wood / Lora S Irish.
    pages cm
Includes index.
ISBN 978-1-56523-478-9 (pbk.)
1. Pyrography. I. Title. II. Title: Art and craft of pyrography.
TT199.8.I74 2012
745.51'4--dc23
                    2012000893

To learn more about the other great books from Fox Chapel Publishing, or to find a retailer near you,
call toll-free 800-457-9112 or visit us at *www.FoxChapelPublishing.com*.

Note to Authors: We are always looking for talented authors to write new books in our area of
woodworking, design, and related crafts. Please send a brief letter describing your idea to
Acquisition Editor, 1970 Broad Street, East Petersburg, PA 17520.

Printed in China
Second printing

About the Author

Lora S. Irish is an internationally known artist and author, whose acclaimed books include:

101 Artistic Relief Patterns

Classic Carving Patterns

Easy & Elegant Beaded Copper Jewelry

Great Book of Celtic Patterns

Great Book of Dragon Patterns

Great Book of Fairy Patterns

Great Book of Floral Patterns

Great Book of Tattoo Designs

Great Book of Woodburning

Modern Tribal Tattoo Designs

North American Wildlife Patterns for the Scroll Saw

Relief Carving Wood Spirits

The Official Vampire Artist's Handbook

Wildlife Carving in Relief

Wood Spirits and Green Men

World Wildlife Patterns for the Scroll Saw

Lora S. Irish

In addition to her work as an author, in 1997, working from her home studio, Lora and her husband, Michael, created www.carvingpatterns.com, an Internet-based studio focusing on online tutorials, projects, and patterns created exclusively by Lora for crafters and artisans. The website offers more than 1,500 patterns in various subject categories, including Americana, Animal and Wildlife, Celtic Knots, Dragons and Beasts, Nautical and Sea Life, Spirit People, and many more. Lora continues to provide new patterns—and inspiration to many artists—at the site.

Lora also contributes a regular relief carving pattern column to *Woodcarving Illustrated* magazine and is a frequent contributor to *Scroll Saw Woodworking and Crafts* magazine.

Acknowledgments

Thanks, as always, to Fox Chapel Publisher Alan Giagnocavo and Editorial Director John Kelsey, who offer great support to my new ideas for books. Alan has always encouraged me to explore new ideas, new techniques, and new crafts, never limiting the path where each new book takes me. Fox Chapel's willingness to explore new ideas and new arts for book manuscripts has accentuated my growth as a craft artist.

Special thanks are extended to Paul Hambke and the entire Fox editorial team for their outstanding support and input.

I also would like to thank the design team at Fox Chapel—art director Troy Thorne and designer Jason Deller, in particular. That team is responsible for the superb look and wonderful layout of this book.

Special thanks goes out to the sales and marketing team and the customer service reps at Fox.

My most lasting gratitude goes to my husband, Michael. Through thirty-three years of marriage and twenty-five years as a working team, he has endured reams of art paper, piles of craft supplies, tons of paint tubes and brushes, and a home that can smell like turpentine or linseed oil, all with a prideful delight in his wife's accomplishments. He has suffered through eating microwave dinners on TV trays because the kitchen table was full of the latest projects and through my creative tantrums when I have too many projects going at the same time.

Contents

PART ONE

Basic Supplies

Basic Supply List:

- Single-temperature solid-tip tool
- Variable-temperature units
- Standard writing tip pen
- Micro writing tip pen
- Medium or spoon shader tip pen
- Sandpaper
- Sanding pads, 220 to 320 grit
- Foam core fingernail files
- Emery cloth or silicon carbide cloth
- Fine steel wool
- Leather strop, strop rouge
- Pencils
- Colored ink pen
- Carbon or graphite paper
- Transparent tape
- White artist eraser
- Transparent tape
- Dusting brush

- Old tooth brush
- Assorted soft painting brushes
- Ceramic tile
- Rulers and straight edge
- T-square or right angle triangle
- Cardboard or chipboard
- Canvas stretchers
- Long quilter's straight pins
- Bench knife or utility knife
- X-acto knife
- Small round gouge
- Acrylic spray sealer
- White glue
- Hot glue gun
- Fabric paint
- Artist colored pencils
- Watercolor pencils

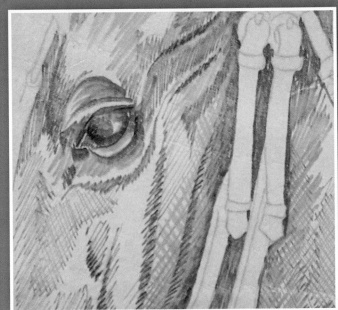

Pyrography Systems

There are two types of pyrography systems—the one-temperature unit and the variable-temperature system.

One-temperature tools heat to a pre-set temperature and create tonal value by controlling your texture or burn strokes and by the speed of your burning stroke.

Variable-temperature tools allow you to adjust the temperature of the tips from a very cool setting to extremely hot.

The numbers of distinct tonal values that can easily be created increases with the variable temperature tool because you control how cool or hot the tip is during the work.

Options. From single- to variable-temperature units, pyrographers can choose from many options. Your skill level, your goals as an artist or craftsman, and your budget are among the factors that will influence your decision.

Horse Portrait Practice Board Pattern

The *Horse Portrait Practice Board Pattern* was worked on the end scrap for the larger leather burning *Civil War Generals* (see page 114).

Measuring 3" wide by 12" (76mm by 31cm) high, the leather scrap provided enough room to create a long, narrow design.

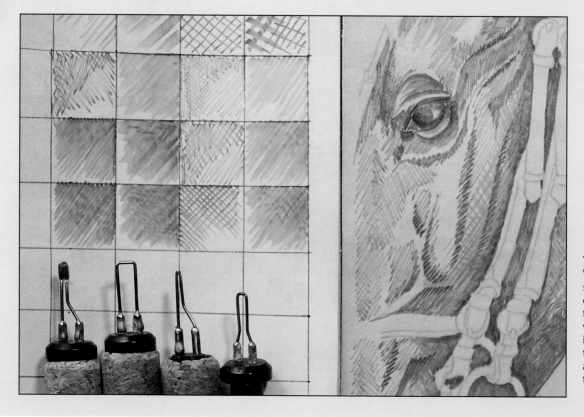

Tip variety. Woodburning systems, whether one-temperature fixed-tip tools or variable-temperature interchangeable-pen tools, come with a variety of pen tip profiles.

One-temperature tools

Once plugged into an electrical outlet the tool quickly reaches an even but high temperature so the textures you make, strokes that you use, and the speed of the stroke control the tonal value work in your project.

Using a light pressure to the tip against the wood and moving the tool tip quickly through the burn stroke creates very pale tonal values. Medium pressure and slower motion bring darker tones. One-temperature burning tools are inexpensive, readily available at your local craft or hobby store and excellent for first-time pyrographers to give the craft a try.

Pen types. Pens with interchangeable tips (separated unit above) allow you to increase your inventory of tip shapes without spending a lot of money. Fixed-tip pens (blue grip above) eliminate any heat or energy loss where the interchangeable tip connects with the unit.

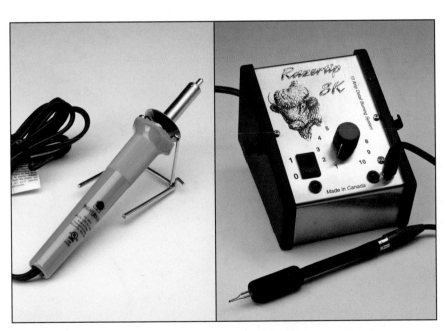

Temperature control. The single-temperature burner on the left takes time to heat up but holds its temperature well. The variable-temperature burner on the right heats up—and cools—quickly.

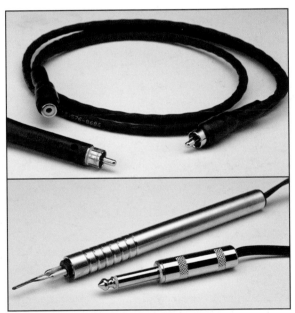

Handpiece wires. Most woodburners use an RCA plug (top photo) to connect the burning pen to the handpiece wire. Some units (bottom photo) use a ¼"-diameter phone jack for the connection.

Variable-temperature burners

Variable-temperature systems have a dial thermostat that allows you to control how cool or hot your tip is. You can adjust the temperature setting quickly making it easy to control your tonal values in your project. This style has two types of pens—the fixed tip pen, where the tip is permanently set in the handgrip, and the interchangeable pen, where different wire tips can be used with the handgrip. There are many excellent burning systems available to the hobbyist. Which manufacturer you chose depends on your budget, your pen style preferences, and what is available to you locally or online.

Dual-pen system. With a dual-pen system, plug two pens, each with a different tip, into the unit during any burning session. A selector switch allows the user to change from one pen to the other and a thermostat controls the temperature setting for whichever tip is in use.

The pens for this unit are slim and lightweight, making it comfortable for long sessions of burning. The lead wire that goes from the pen to the burning unit is permanently affixed to the pen's end. The handgrip area may be covered with foam wrap or cork to reduce the heat that reaches the hand.

Single-pen unit. Many single-pen units have a range of temperature settings. Changing fixed pens or changing tips on the interchangeable pens is quick and easy. The temperature dial system is very reliable for quick tonal value changes. This particular unit can reach very hot temperatures and working to the extreme black tones is simply a matter of turning up the heat.

The cork handles are very comfortable and dramatically reduce the heat transfer from the tip to your hand. This style uses a positive, tight connector at the front of the pen for the interchangeable tip pen making the exchange of tips easy.

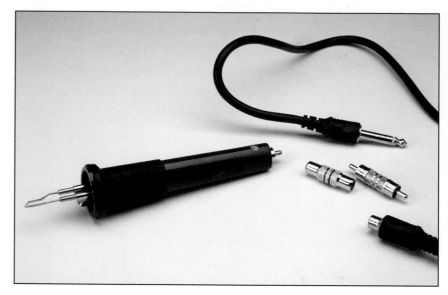

Adaptability. Most manufacturers sell adapters that allow you to use other manufacturers' pens with their control units. Some units come with a full set of adapters.

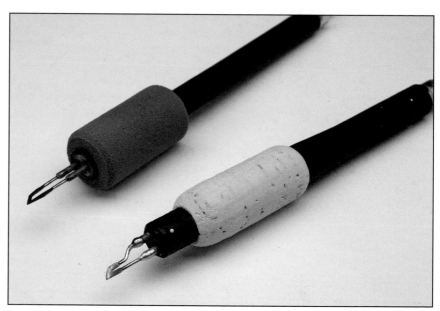

Pen grips. The thick blue foam on the pen above insulates the user's fingers from the heat of the pen. Vents and distance on the pen below move the user's fingers back from the hottest part of the pen.

For more information about pyrography machines, visit the "Pyrography Machine Buyer's Guide" at *www.pyrographyonline.com*

Pyrography tips

Tips comes in many shapes and bends from the tight bend used in the standard writing tip to half circles that can create fish scales and even square tubes that make a textured pattern on your board. Three basic pen tips are used throughout this book—the standard writing tip, the micro writing tip, and a small flat spoon shader.

Standard writing tip pen. For wide line shading and texture work, try the standard writing tip. By holding the pen in an upright position, 90° from the working surface, fine detail lines can be pulled. To create wider lines in your texturing, drop your grip to about 45° from the wood. The angle change allows the side of the wire to touch the board giving you more metal to wood contact.

Standard tip sample. The standard tip pen creates a strong, wide line perfect for both outlining and shading.

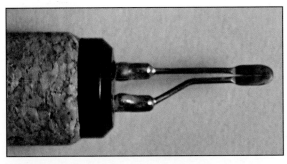

Spoon shader tip pen. This small flat shader creates a wide path of smooth tonal values and is excellent for general shading within your design. Shader tips come in several profiles from spoon shaped, square, and half rounds.

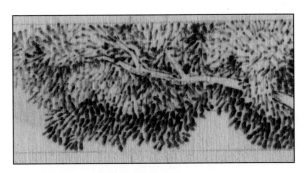

Spoon shader sample. Large areas can quickly be toned using the spoon shaped shading tip.

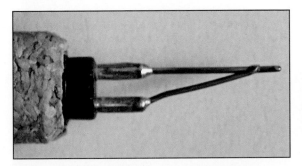

Micro writing tip pen. The micro writing tools is manufactured using thinner wire and a tighter bend at the tip. The tip's shape allows little metal to come into direct contact to the working surface and produces fine detailing lines. Fine dense textures can be layered using this tool to burn an area into an even, smooth tonal value.

Micro tip sample. For extremely fine line work, try the micro tip pen.

General Supplies

You will want to gather a small tool kit of craft supplies for your pyrography. Many of these items are common household items you already may have on hand. Through this section, we will be looking at those supplies and their use in your pyro hobby.

For sanding:

- Sandpaper, from 220 to 320 grit
- Sanding pads
- Foam core fingernail files

Your wood surfaces need a light sanding to create a smooth surface for burning. Use fine-grit sandpaper, 220 to 320, to remove the fine ridges and remove loose fibers on the wood. Coarser sandpaper, lower than 220 grit, can leave sanding lines that can affect how the quality of your burn lines. Even fine ridges will cause your tool tip to skip or move as you pull the stroke resulting in uneven or non-straight lines.

Sanding pads have a foam core and are flexible making them great for curved surfaces as on a wood plate or the routed edge of a plaque. Available at your local drug store foam core fingernail files are a nice addition to your tool kit.

For cleaning tool tips

- Emery cloth or silicon carbide cloth
- Fine steel wool
- Leather strop, strop rouge, red oxide or aluminum oxide

It is important to keep your tool tips well cleaned during any burning session to ensure even heat to the tip and consistent color tones to your burning. As you work, notice the tool tips become dark or dull as carbon from the burning builds up on the wire. The carbon can affect the heat coming from the tip to the wood and leave black carbon smudges on your work. Clean the tips of your tools often.

Smooth surface. Sanding wood surfaces before tracing your pattern onto the medium ensures as smooth a working surface as possible. Paper, cloth, and leather do not require sanding.

Cleaning your tips. There are several methods for cleaning the wire tips of the variable temperature tool.

Scraping the tip with a special tool provided by the manufacturer or with a sharpened knife can quickly clean the tip. Emery cloth , fine steel wool, or a woodcarving leather strop prepared with either red oxide rouge or with aluminum oxide are alternatives.

For tracing:

- Pencils
- Colored ink pen
- Carbon or graphite paper
- Transparent tape

Two products used to transfer the design to your work surface are carbon and graphite papers.

Both products are laid under your paper pattern so that the transfer side is against your work surface. Both should be used carefully as they are not easily removed from your work surface after burning is complete. Graphite paper, with its soft pale grey coloring is especially appropriate for gourds, papier-mâché, and darker woods.

You can also blacken the back of your pattern paper with a soft pencil, covering it completely. Place the pattern onto your work surface and trace over the pattern lines leaving a fine line of pencil graphite on your work surface. The pencil lines can later be removed with a white artist eraser.

And generally...

- White artist eraser
- Transparent tape
- Dusting brush
- Old tooth brush
- Assorted soft painting brushes
- Ceramic tile or wood palette
- Rulers and straight edge
- T square or right angle triangle

- Cardboard
- Canvas stretchers
- Long quilter's straight pins
- Bench knife or utility knife
- X-Acto knife
- Small round gouge

Many common household items and tools are used for pyrography to prepare the working surface, secure your pattern, trace the design, and finish the completed burning.

If you will be adding paint to your finished burning you will need an assortment of soft bristle brushes, a paint palette, water pans, and, of course, the thinning medias whichever type of paint you have chosen to use.

Bench knives or X-Acto knives can be used to carefully carve away small mistakes in the burning and to cut fine highlight lines into an area that has already been burned. Some pyrographers also use them as scrapers to clean the tool tips.

When working on cotton canvas you will want several sheets of heavy cardboard and long quilter's straight pins to secure the cloth so that you are working on a tight, non-moving surface. Canvas stretchers can be purchased at your local art store so that you can secure large pieces of canvas fabric.

Also include in your kit white artist erasers. Please avoid pink erasers as they can leave pink streaks of color on your work surface that is not easily removed. The white eraser cleans up any left over tracing lines and any oil or dirt from your hands that builds up during a burning session.

Large dusting brushes are excellent to remove the dust created during the preparations stage of sanding your wood surface. Old toothbrushes can also be used; they also are useful in removing any excess rouge from your tool tips during preparation.

PART TWO

Practice Boards

New designs or patterns present new challenges for you as a pyrographer. Each working surface has its own texture, density, and color tone that affect the evenness and final look of each burn stroke. By working a small scrap of the same material you can experiment with your pyrography ensure the best burn possible on your larger project.

A practice board will be used to record your tonal values according to your temp settings. With each new step in your pyrography project, do a small sample burning on your practice board making any necessary adjustments to tip, texture, and temperature before putting pen to project.

As you explore each working surface available to pyrographers, you will find small projects that you can use as your practice session works.

Five factors determine the final look of any area of burning. As you work your practice board make note of each of these directly on your grid so that you can, at will, reproduce any of your textures or stroke fill patterns:

- Working surface
- Tool tip profile
- Temperature setting
- Fill or texture pattern
- Hand position

Practice boards do not need to be scraps of your working surface—they can become full-fledged projects of their own. This papier-mâché grocery bag was the practice board for the Sunflower Yarn Caddy project.

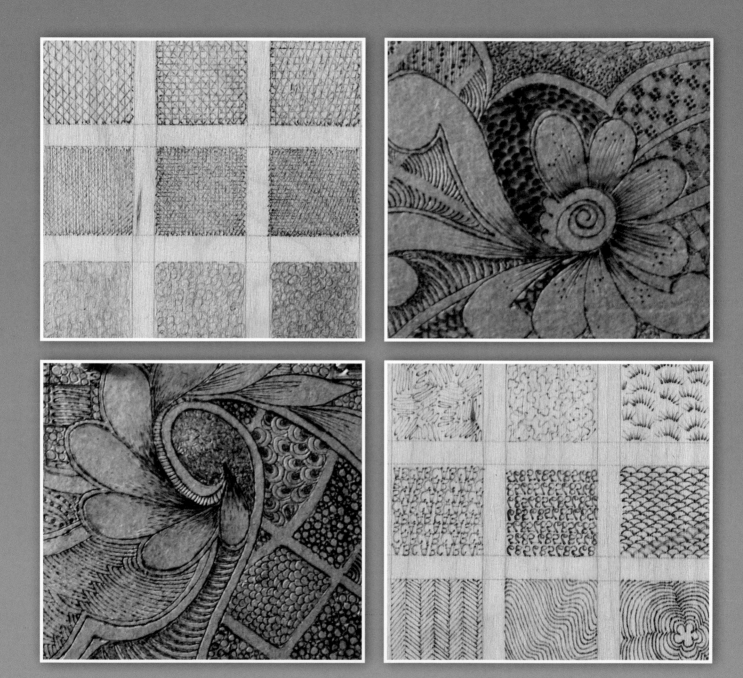

Creating a Wood Practice Board

The most basic practice board—the one I recommend all beginning pyrographers create—is laid out as a grid pattern on a large sheet of birch or poplar plywood. This practice board can be used repeatedly to test your temperature settings, try new pen tip strokes, and to create new textures.

Temperature settings

In the example (below left), my first row (right row A) I set the burner temp setting at 5 and then filled the top square with a random curling doodle stroke. The square below it was worked on setting 6, then setting 7 through to setting 9. With each temperature change the tonal value becomes darker. I have marked my temperature setting in pencil to the right of each square for easy reference later.

Creating textures. Mark a 10" x 12" (254mm x 305mm) sheet of poplar or birch plywood or a piece of basswood into five rows of 1" (25mm) squares with a pencil. Use the grid squares to create each new texture.

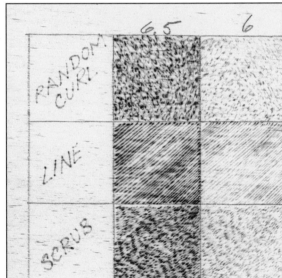

Marking the board. Make pencil notations on your practice board for both the temperature setting and pen tip used.

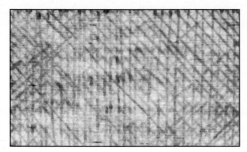
Crosshatch Texture

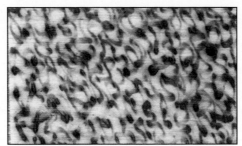
Random Doodle

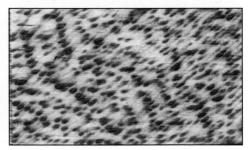
Scrubbie Stroke

Three common fill patterns

Three common fill patterns used in pyrography are crosshatching, random doodles, and the scrubbie stroke.

Crosshatching fills an area with layers of fine parallel lines. Each new layer is laid on a diagonal to the last, slowly developing the depth of the tonal value.

Make the **random doodle stroke** by working tightly packed loops. As the new looping line crosses an older line, the area becomes denser and therefore darker.

The **scrubbie** is a short back-and-forth stroke that quickly fills an area. The space between each of those back-and-forth strokes, how much unburned area is allowed, establishes your tonal depth.

As you work your practice board you will discover the fill strokes that are the most comfortable or natural for you to use in your style of work.

These pages show you how to set up your own basic practice board using wood.

In this book, I've taken practice boards a step further and show you how to create boards that are projects all on their own and not just the standard grid pattern.

Additional practice board examples using different media, appear:

Project	Medium	Page
Horse Portrait	leather	pages 10, 30–31, 33
Grocery Bag	papier mâché	pages 16, 80
Free motion quilting	wood	page 23
Southwest birdhouse	gourd	page 47
Posies Practice	chipboard	page 61
Native American Bead Rattle	gourd	pages 62–64
Steampunk	chipboard	page 67
Christmas ornaments	chipboard	page 68
Paper dragon	paper	page 88
Seed bags	cloth	page 91
Bengal tiger	wood	pages 99–101

Hand positions

How you hold your pen tip in relationship to the working surface directly affects the width and darkness of the stroke. While you are working your practice board, try several different hand positions using the same pen tip, temperature setting, and texture fill pattern.

1 Grip area. Variable-temperature burning system pens come with a grip area that keeps your fingertips well away from the hot wire end.

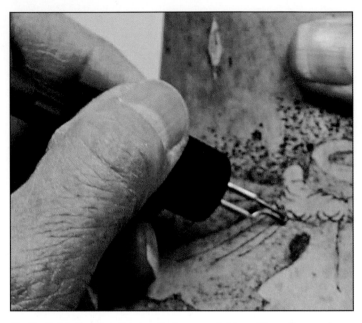

2 Upright. Holding the pen tip in an upright position allows only the very point or top edge of the tip to touch your work. This creates fine lines or fine shading strokes.

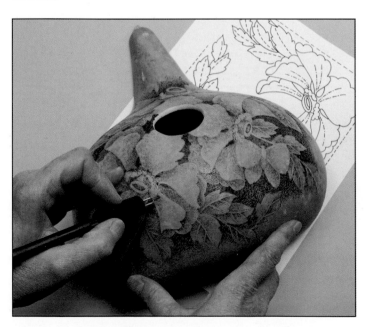

3 Standard grip. Hold your pen exactly as you would an ink pen, using a comfortable writing position.

4 More contact. Laying the pen tip into a lower, closer to the surface, position allows more of the pen wire to contact the surface and therefore creates darker, wider burn strokes.

Tool tips

The profile of your pen tip, obviously, affects both the width of the line you burn as well as what type of texture or stroke patterns that is most appropriate to that tip.

As you work your practice board, try each tip profile that you have for each of the texture and fill strokes that you may be using on your project.

A crosshatch pattern made with the micro writing tip will create a pale, thin lined, open checkering design. Using the standard writing tip that same crosshatching will look like a pen and ink illustration with bolder lines. Wide basket-weave strokes are made using a spoon or square shader and that same crosshatch fill pattern.

1 Standard tip. The standard writing tip provides a medium-sized line that can easily handle temperature ranges from extremely pale through almost black toned burns.

2 Medium square. The shader tip makes large, wide strokes, best used for even colored fill areas. A medium square shader is shown here.

3 Micro writer. With its extra-fine point, the micro writer can be used to create extremely fine, pale tonal textures, adding names and dates, and used to create a fine line outline stroke.

Common texture and stroke patterns

In the two close-ups of the *Blue Jay Mill* (right, and opposite page), you may see a blue jay sitting on an oak branch with leaves and acorns or a stone mill with a small lean-to addition.

Looking closer you will discover there are no shading strokes—no smooth, blended areas of work that gradually changed sepia tones. Instead, both of these samples were worked strictly with texturing strokes.

Create the blue jay using all fine detail line work. Work the pale tonal values in the beak, around the eye, and in the belly area at a low setting using tightly packed short lines.

Medium-length lines at a medium-temperature setting establish the top of the head, back area above the wings, and the base of the tail.

Working with tightly packed short lines and a hot temperature the markings around the eyes, on the wings, and on the tail complete the bird.

Blue jay closeup.

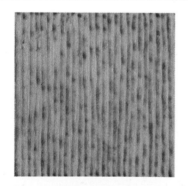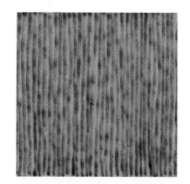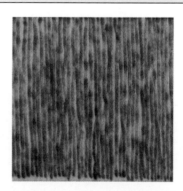

Fine line textures.

Crosshatching was used throughout the mill complex for this pattern. It is most defined in the chimney—worked with just a few crossover layers of fine lines. The sides of the mill were darkened in tonal value with the addition of more crosshatch layers.

Create the background trees using a spoon shader tip on a low-temperature setting and wide "touch-and-pull" strokes. Use "touch-and-lift" strokes made with a small spoon shader to create the foreground.

Refer to your practice board often for ideas on how any area of your burning can be developed.

Mill closeup.

Free motion quilting practice board. An area of your work can be created using the fill stroke previously discussed. They can also be fill using small repetitive textures. In this sample, worked from a free-motion quilting pattern, each area has a small pattern design from small tightly packed circles, checkerboard squares, flower petals, and even fish scales.

PART THREE

Surfaces & Projects

Pyrographers are not constrained to wood. Any media that is grown or made from natural fibers and is free of toxic chemicals can be burned. A few ideas are gourds, cotton canvas, rag content artist paper, leather, chipboard, and papier-mâché. We will take a quick look at each in this chapter then focus on each burning surface through a step-by-step project.

Because all of our working surfaces are natural products, they will contain small imperfections that can affect the evenness or smoothness of your burn. Wood surfaces have varying grain patterns. For some woods, the grain line will burn to a darker tonal value than the non-grain lines. Papier-mâché—a compressed glued shredded paper product—will have areas that burn more quickly than other areas creating a mottled effect. Variations in any burning caused by the natural surface are common and simply a part of our art.

Any natural fiber surface that is unfinished and chemical-free may be used as your pyrography substrate or working surface. (Clockwise from top left: wood, vegetable-tanned leather, cotton canvas, and papier-mâché.)

Vegetable-Tanned Leather

Vegetable tanned, non-dyed leather is a favorite burning media for many pyrographers. Available in large pieces, pre-cut kits, and pre-manufactured forms including purses, book covers, and wallets, leather offers a world of three-dimensional possibilities.

Leather comes in a variety of weights from lightweight 1 ounce leather, which is approximately 1/64" (.5mm) thick, to 7–8 ounces, which is 1/8" (3mm) thick, to even heavier belt-weight leathers, which can be a 1/4" (6mm) thick. The weight or thickness of the leather that you chose depends on the use and shape of your final project. The sample used for this lesson is worked on 1/4" (6mm) belt weight leather from a tanned side.

Leather in pre-dyed colors and suede textures is also available, but neither is recommended for burning. The chemicals used to pre-finish and pre-dye leather can create toxic fumes during burning. Suede leather does not provide the smooth, controllable surface for clean, clear burned lines.

Soft surface

Leather has a soft surface and the pressure of a pencil tracing a pattern on its surface often creates indentations. Use as light a pressure as possible with your tracing ink pen during the transfer process. Once the design has been traced and the pattern paper removed, strengthen your tracing lines by penciling over any light or missing areas. The pencil lines can be erased after the burning is completed.

As you work your leather project, you will discover that the woodburning tip will physically sculpture and shape your design, adding dimension to your tonal work. Run your hand across your burning and feel the ridges of the unburned areas and valleys your burning tool creates. Use this property of leather to give your finished burning a relief carved effect, using the woodburning tips and temperature setting to physically distinguish one area of the pattern from another.

Because of the soft nature of leather, begin burning at low temperatures. Leather burns quickly and tends to go directly to the mid-tone color range. Using a very low temperature setting early in your work will help you avoid losing the light, pale tones in your design. For my mapping stage, I work at a setting of 3 as compared to a setting of 5 to 6 to develop the same pale tonal values on birch plywood.

Dark chocolate and black tones are developed using a simple touch-and-lift spot burning. In my experience leather seldom burns to a true black tone, dark tones often stop in the deep brown range. Please be careful using high temperature settings— it is possible to burn completely through a piece of leather, especially thinner leather under 1/8" thick.

Vegetable-tanned leather may have small imperfections that can effect your burning. Be prepared to discover thin areas in the leather, small scratches and dents, and even field brands.

Olson's Dairy Truck. Creating stunning, realistic pyrography scenes requires only a variable-temperature burning unit, a few pen tips, a working surface, and a few common household tools and supplies.

Civil War Generals

(Uses pattern on page 114.)

History in leather. Civil War generals James Longstreet (left) and Robert E. Lee.

Supplies:

- 12" (31cm) square vegetable tanned leather
- Standard writing tip
- Spoon shader tip
- Medium square shader tip
- 12" x 12" (31cm x 31cm) chipboard
- Contact cement
- Graphite paper

1 Prepare your burning surface. Cut the leather using a bench knife. Leather does not need any surface prep but if I am working a large flat piece of leather not destined to become part of a project such as a carry bag or purse, I like to glue the leather to chipboard. Leather tends to curl both because it is often shipped rolled, and because of the temperature changes to the leather during the burning process. Chipboard eliminates some—not all—of this tendency.

2 Attach chipboard backing. I have cut my leather to a 12" (31cm) square. Using wood glue or contact cement, I attach the chipboard to the back of the leather. A large stack of books will act as a clamp while the glue dries. Usually I will wait until the next day to begin burning.

Horse Portrait Practice Board

(Uses pattern on page 112.)

Limiting practice boards to fill-in-the-block grids or small unusable scraps of your project surface is sometimes a missed opportunity.

This *Horse Portrait Practice Board* has been worked on a 3" wide by 12" long (76mm by 31cm) piece of vegetable-tanned leather. When it was completed, I glued the practice board to a large 12" (31cm) square of corkboard to create a memo board gift for an equine-loving friend.

Sometimes you may want to practice an actual portion of the project pattern that you will be working or some specific design element. You can treat practice areas in the project exactly as you would any other practice board surface—as a sample work that allows you to make mistakes, make changes, and even completely rework areas of a pattern.

For my practice board sample for leather, because I am not experienced with horses or riding, I wanted a chance to explore how a bridle was constructed and strapped, and how it lays on the animal's face. Shown here are the first two burning stages for pale and mid-tone values.

Looking at the practice board, you can see that different texture strokes are used to create the shadows in the horse's face—crosshatching, lightly and densely packed areas of straight line work, and wide stroke lines made with the spoon shader.

In the early stages of work, this particular practice board was turning out so well that I made my temperature setting and tool tip notes on another scrap.

Being bold with both the pattern design and scrap surfaces when you are laying out your practice board may result in two wonderful pyrography projects completed instead of just one.

See page 10 on "Pyrography Systems" for a photo of the accompanying grid piece.

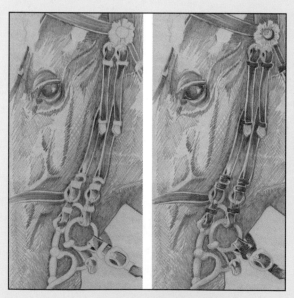

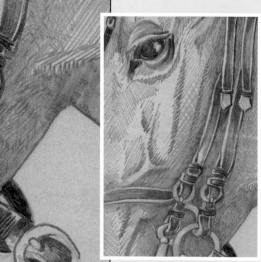

Practice board. The first (left) and second (right) burn layers for the Civil War Generals Project. (Please see the Civil War Generals step-by-step project instructions for progress images of this practice board.)

The third burning layer.

3 **Trace the pattern.** Once the leather and board's glue were set I transferred my pattern to the leather using graphite paper and a hard 8H pencil. A hard pencil gives me a fine line tracing. Graphite does not completely erase from the leather so fine lines are less likely to appear after the burning. When the transfer set is complete I rubbed the entire leather surface with a dry eraser pad, which you can pick up at a drafting supply store. It is simply finely ground eraser particles in a cloth bag. Erasing now lightens the graphite lines before I begin to burn.

4 **Test textures and strokes.** On a scrap from the same hide that I will be using for my main project, I have inked a ¾" x ¾" (19mm x 19mm) grid. The right-hand row is worked with my narrow square shader, the second with the standard writing tip, the third with the wide square shader, and the fourth (left row) used my spoon shader. All of these burnings were done at a temperature setting of 1.5.

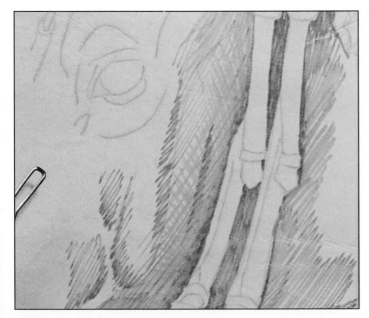

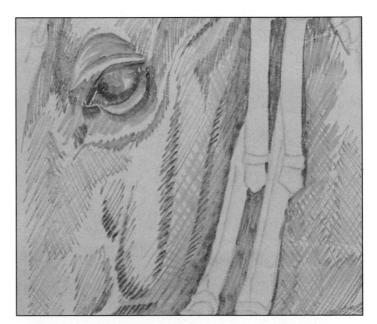

5 **Burning pale tones.** I want a pale tonal value for my fighting soldiers in the Civil War scene, so I set my temperature setting at 1.5 and use my narrow square shader and standard writing tip and quick, relaxed strokes to begin a practice burn of the horse's flesh area. Photography was a new technology at the start of the Civil War. However, the technology was limited and photographers needed to set the scene, set the camera, and then take a long exposure to achieve a clear photo. There are staged photos of battles, but no actual battle photos.

6 **Stroke patterns.** Newspapers and journals during the Civil War era depended on sketch artists. Some sketches became engravings for the daily journals. Sketch artists used quick, coarse strokes to capture the general scene and later cleaned the sketches up. I want the same effect for the horse, bridle, and main background. I use my narrow shader, first on the wide flat edge to create the dark, solid tones surrounding the bridle leathers and then on the corner to create the finer lines that imply shading in the horse's face.

7 **Working the background scene.** Work the background scene of soldiers, corn stalks, and fence in as soft and pale a tonal value as possible. More detailing or shading can be added later.

8 **First background layer.** I worked my background soldiers with quick doodle strokes using my standard writing tip. With a few roughly worked areas and little change in the tonal value, the soldiers begin to take form and shape. The soldier behind Longstreet and the ground upon which he kneels are all shaded. That shading stops at the profile line for Longstreet's face.

9 **Covering graphite lines.** I have changed my tip to my micro writing tip but am still using a temperature setting of 1.5. Because the graphite tracing lines on leather do not erase completely, I have worked through the soldiers to burn thin scratchy lines where the graphite lines are obvious.

10 **Adding the fence and corn.** The corn, fence and little more ground area have now been worked. I used my narrow square shader, first on the flat to work the leaves then on the corner to create the wood grain lines in the fence. With the soldier background worked I am going to return to my practice pattern horse bridle to discover where my mid-tones will be with both tips and temperature.

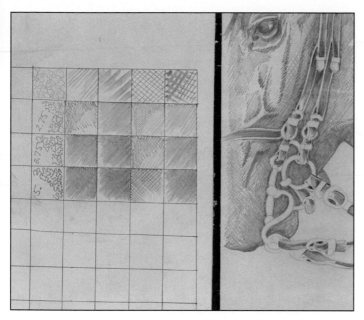

11 **Add a second practice board layer.** I have returned to my practice grid and practice pattern to determine the temperature range for mid-tones and darks. For my burner, a setting of 2 gives a medium tonal range. That value has been added to the leather portions of the bridle using my standard writing tip. After one layer of work a second layer deepens the curved areas of the leather using the standard writing tip and a setting of 3. Turning the temperature down to near 0 and using the standard writing tip gives an extremely light tone to the metal rings, especially around the horse's mouth.

12 **Temperature setting for dark tones.** A setting of 5 burns very dark areas. Using my spoon shader, I added deep tones to the upper bridle area. A few very dark lines, all worked on the right side of the bridle leather, crisp the leatherwork. Using the edge of my spoon shader and the 5 setting, I worked the horse's hair in a random doodle stroke.

13 **The generals' faces.** A pale shading accents the faces under the hat brims, along the outer cheek lines, and at the beginnings of the beards, as in General James Longstreet (left). For General Robert E. Lee (right) I worked with my standard writing tip at a setting of 0 to 1 to ensure a soft pale tone burn for the shading along the sides, noses, and brow lines of the two faces.

14 **Adding mid-tones to the faces.** Mid-tone shading accents the eyes of both men. Black tones will soon be added. For Lee's face (right), using my micro writing tip and a setting of 2 to 3, I added a few dark areas—the eye pupils, the upper eye lid line, the brow line, the nostrils, and several points inside the ears.

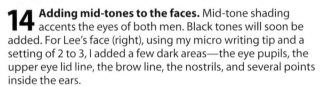

15 **Facial hair.** Returning to my standard tip and the 0–1 temperature setting, I have worked a second shading layer in the faces where the hat brims overset the brow. With my micro tip and temperature setting at 3, I work the beginnings of the beards.

16 **Longstreet's beard, hat, and coat.** I added dark tones to the generals' beards and hair using the sharp edge of the spoon shader at a hot temperature setting. Working on Longstreet's clothing, I set my temperature at 0–1 for pale tones, 2–3 for medium tones, and moved it up to 3.5 for dark tones. I did most of the work using my standard writing tip and a fairly fast, even motion to give a smooth shading effect. I began with a soft, pale tone shading with most of the work on your right side of his coat.

17 **Developing the coat's shadows.** Still working your right side, even though this is Longstreet's darkest area, it still has changes in the tonal value where the coat and pants roll or fold. The inside area of the left side coat collar is also in the very dark tones. The final layer of shading adds the folds to the left side of the coat, where his arm touches the left side of the coat, his belt, and the trim on his sleeve and leather gloves.

18 **Working Lee's hat and coat.** I have now worked through Lee's clothing in the same manner. The second layering establishes the folds, the vest area, and his shirt.

19 **Adding dark tones.** The darkest tones fall in the right side of Lee's coat, along his neck line in the shirt and vest, and some extra shading where belly area falls behind the hand and reins.

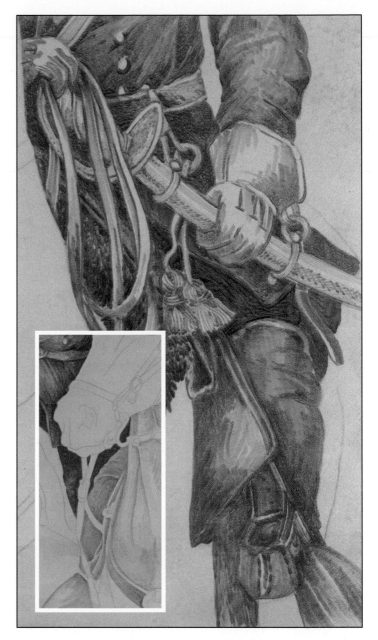

20 **Changing Lee's facial expression.** The leather gloves, sword metal, and sword cords are all worked in pale to medium tones, which contrasts them with the black tones of the coat and pushes them forward. I knew my Lee had a smile but decided to wait and develop the areas around the face before I did any corrections. Lee's smile comes from three areas—the front curve of his eyebrow, a crow's foot wrinkle at the outer corner of the eye, and from a mustache line at the outer corner of his mouth. I used a bench knife to carefully cut away these areas. The top edge of the eyebrow now has a slight dip. The crow's foot has been reduced and now pushes down the outer corner of the eye where before the eye corner lifted with the wrinkle. I removed all of mustache line above the outer lip corner. I will not re-burn these areas! Because the tanned surface of the leather in these three areas has been removed, those areas will not burn to the same tonal value as the surrounding areas. Instead, I will leave them in the white of the leather.

21 **Working Lee's hand, sword, and left leg.** I have worked down through Lee's pants and boots using a temperature setting above 3. The leather of the saddle, saddle blanket, and woolskin are also worked in hotter temperatures, which allows the bridle reins in Lee's hand to be worked in the mid-tone ranges and pushes the reins in front of Lee's body. Begin work on Lee's right leg using a low temperature shading and my spoon shader tip. Bring up the detailing and the darker shadows with a slightly higher temperature setting. By starting the entire area in a mid-tone burn, I keep the straps from the saddle, bridle, and Lee's leather boots darker than his horse's neck and face areas.

23 **Leather flaws.** Working in the lowest area of the leather using a low burning temperature to begin developing the horses, I brought up a flaw in the leather surface (left). You can see it as two stripes that run horizontal from just below the nose of Longstreet's horse to the chest of Lee's horse. When the flaw began to show, I lowered my temperature settings to zero and gently used a large flat shader tip across the entire lower area. This let me see the flaw, because these two areas are burning a slight tonal value deeper than the surrounding areas. For me, this is not a major flaw or even a problem with this burning. Leather is a natural product and does have areas that burn differently than surrounding surfaces. By using the very low burn, however, I can see exactly where the flaw lines fall and be ready to compensate for their presence.

22 **Between the horses.** The area between the two horses contains Longstreet's left leg and Lee's right leg. A dark-toned burn establishes Longstreet's leg. Moving to a slightly cooler setting puts Lee's leg in front of Longstreet by using medium-dark tones.

24 **Horse colors.** Lee's horse, Traveler, was pale gray toned with darker gray markings around the muzzle and forehead areas of the face with a dark gray to black mane and tail. There is at least one photo of this horse, who outlived his master by a few years. Longstreet's horse was noted as a dark bay, so I have done a light overall tone that will become the medium highlights after the dark shading is added.

25 **Traveler's facial shadows.** Working back and forth between the two horses I have added some shading to Traveler's face.

26 **Finding the focus.** I want the focus on the two men—I want the background there but not prominent. I want that same effect for the horses so I have returned to a more illustrative, scrubbie type stroke using my standard writing tip.

27 **Traveler's mane and eyes.** The eyes of Traveler and his nostrils have been deepened and the gray mussel coloring added. His mane was added using my spoon shader on the side (sharp) edge at a medium-hot setting. Longstreet's horse now has more definition to his muscles and facial areas. Longstreet's horse's belly, between the two horses—Longstreet's leg and Lee's leg—has been brought to a deep medium tone with black toned shadows. This forces the horse's belly back into the design and back to the same visual plane as the men's legs.

28 **Adding Longstreet's horse's facial features.** The addition of the dark tones in Longstreet's horse's face and the shadowing around his bridle area is worked. More shading has been added in his belly area, especially below the saddle blanket.

29 **Leatherwork bridles.** The final step is to work the leather of the bridles on both horses. I chose a medium tone and the scrubbie, illustrative-type stroke.

Blue Jay Mill

(Uses pattern on page 116.)

1 **Barn wall shading.** The Blue Jay Mill is worked on an 11" wide by 14" high (28cm by 36cm) piece of ⅞ ounce leather. I rubbed the back of the pattern paper with a soft #2 pencil, placed the paper on the leather, and then traced the design on using an ink pen. I burned the design as if it were a rough pencil sketch, allowing the lines of the burning strokes to define many of the areas and elements in the design. In the first step, I used my standard writing tip to create the shading in the barn walls, tree trunks, and fine long pine needles in the mid-ground trees, the grassy ridges, and in the oak leaves. A large spear or spoon shader was used to create the background trees, stones in the barn walls, and the water reflections. The barn roofs, much of the grass, the water below the reflection, and the sky remain unworked giving the pattern a large amount of white tonal value. The undersides of the roofs, the shadows the roofs cast on the walls, the window glass, and the markings in the blue jay are all areas worked to the darkest, or blackest, values in the pattern.

2 **Foreground leaf shading.** In the second stage of the burning, I increased the black and white contrast in the barn by darkening the shading on its walls and adding fine detailing in those shadows. For the front walls of the small lean-to addition of the barn and the wall containing the chimney, I used a textured crosshatch stroke. By increasing the detailing in the stones in the sidewalls, I create more visual contrast to the smooth, untouched white areas of the roofs. I separated the top edges of the roofs from the white unworked area of the sky by fully working the trees behind the barn roofs. This tree line also uses a large amount of texturing created by the large spoon shader tool tip. I burned all of the trees—including the two trees to the left of the barn—in the pale tone range. This pale tone work keeps this area from having any strong black to white contrast.

3 **Adding final details.** In the foreground elements with the tree branch, oak leaves, acorns, and blue jay, there are no pure white highlights and few pale tonal values. The leaves and branches have been shaded but the shading stops in the deep mid-tones. The only true black areas are in the blue jay's wing markings, the shadow he casts on the branch, and in one of the acorn caps. By keeping the elements in the foreground in the middle range of shading values, I reduce the amount of contrast that would attract attention. To keep the roof lines and dark cast shadows in the barn dominant, I reduced the amount of black and white contrast in the other elements and areas in this pattern. By making the background elements pale in value and all of the foreground elements in the deep mid-tone range, the viewer's eye is directed to the harsh black and white contrast found in the barn complex. (See close-up photos pages 22 and 23.)

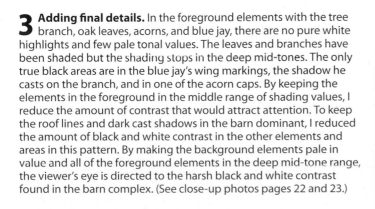

Duck Pond Farm

(Uses pattern on page 117.)

1 **Pale tonal burn.** I cut my project piece from a vegetable-tanned side, approximately ¼" (6mm) thick, to the size of 13" wide by 16¼" high (33cm by 41cm). I allowed the rough edge of the leather hide to become the bottom edge of my project. This particular piece of leather is a second, not the top-quality hide that would be used for a purse or book cover. I chose it because of the distressed wrinkles and spotting as the leather's rough texture added to the feeling of the old country barn landscape. I transferred the pattern to the leather by rubbing the back of the paper pattern with a soft #6 pencil, laying the penciled-covered side of the paper to the leather, and then tracing along the outlines of the pattern. I have used my wide, flat shader tip to establish the flow of the mountains, land ridges, and the water in the creek that runs through the center of the design. My standard writing tip gave me the fine line shading for my barns, fence line, and duck feather groups.

2 **Medium tonal burn.** For the second stage of burning, I turned up my temperature setting slightly to a 4 to 5 level. There are three focal areas in this design—the bank barn in the background area, the springhouse in the mid-ground, and the trio of ducks in the foreground. Two of those focal points—the bank barn and springhouse—are united or linked together by the creek bed. The creek leads your eye from the background barn to the foreground springhouse. The third focal point—the flying ducks—hang in the air above the very important creek bed line. The ducks become visually united to the springhouse when the leaves are added to the foreground tree. During this second stage, I established the darkest tonal areas in my three focal points, including the roof overhangs in the bank barn and springhouse, the windows and doors, and along the shadow sides of the silos. I have added dark tones to the creek bed, grass ridges, and the detailing of the duck feathers.

3 **More medium tones.** For the third stage of the project, I kept the temperature setting from 4 to 5 to continue working in the darker tones and detailing. Along with slightly darkening the foreground grass ridges, I added grass lines and small dark shadows under the grass ridges where they touch the creek. I worked fine line detailing throughout the design including adding barn board lines, roof shingles, grass clusters and texturing to the tree trunks. The fine lines required both my standard writing tip and my small spoon shader tip.

4 **Dark burns and detailing.** During the final stage of burning, I added a background tree line behind the bank barn roof and worked it to a mid-tone value. This darker value in the new trees creates a strong contrast to the white, sun lit roof on the barn, making the roofline more distinct. At the same time, I darkened the trees to the left side of the silos to keep them in the same tonal range as the trees worked for the barn roof. The grass ridges for the bank barn have been darken as well as all of the grass ridge areas from the split rail fence forward. By darkening the entire area, I brought the land area forward in the design. The closer an object is to the viewer the more distinct the shading becomes. Just as I needed to darken the trees to make the bank barn roof show, I needed to darken the leaves in the foreground tree to push the ducks forward in the design. A heavy dark line under each duck also helps to separate the ducks' bodies and wings from the tree leaves.

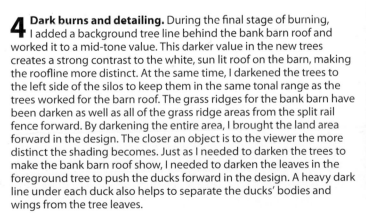

Dried Gourds

With their densely packed wood-like fibers, dried gourds provide pyrographers with interesting shapes to decorate. Easily cut with a craft knife or bench knife, gourds become bowls, sand candle cups, vases, lamps, or delightful birdhouses.

Not all gourds come pre-cleaned and you may need to remove the skin from the outer surface. As the gourd dries, mold blackens the skin. Wear a dust mask whenever working the preparation steps. Latex or rubber gloves will protect your skin for the dust. Soak the gourd in a warm water bath that has several tablespoons of Clorox added. Depending on the thickness of the skin layer, this bath may take up to one-half hour. Roll the gourd often so that there is an even layer of water on its outside.

With a plastic kitchen scrubbie, gently work the skin off. I often find that I need to soak then scrub several times to remove the entire layer. When you have the shell area exposed, allow the gourd to dry. You are ready to cut the gourd with a sharp bench knife, a woodcarving tool, or with a strong utility knife, and to scrape out the seeds from the inside area.

To create an absolute straight line across the surface of a gourd as a cutting guideline, fill your sink or bathtub two-thirds full of water. Set the uncut gourd into the basin and submerge the gourd to the depth that you want your line. When you remove your gourd, you will have a wet line mark across the gourd's surface that is perfectly straight. You can now run a pencil along that wet line as your cutting mark.

Gourds provide pyrographers with a delightful selection of shapes that are easily adaptable to craft projects. Turn bushel basket gourds into large storage containers, canteen gourds into birdhouses, and kettle gourds into cachepots for the greenhouse.

A simple dried gourd can be easily cut into a birdhouse, pitcher, vase, or jewelry box. Once a hole is cut, remove the the inside fibers. Scrape the fibers and seeds out through the hole.

After the seeds have been removed, fill the inside of the gourd with water and allow the gourd to sit for several minutes to moisten the remaining fibers. Continue scraping the inside with your spoon edge until the inside surface is as smooth and clean as the outside. Allow the gourd to dry thoroughly before you begin your project. Again, please use a dust mask when cleaning out the inside of any gourd.

Beyond the basic cleaning and scraping steps, gourds need no special preparation for wood burning. Once burned, a gourd project does not require any finishing spray to seal the gourd surface.

Continuous pattern. The bears, taken from three different pattern drawings, are burned on a leather-covered gourd drum. The pattern is worked in a circular—continuous—pattern around the gourd. (Uses patterns on pages 118–121.)

Southwest Birdhouse—A Practice Board Project

(Uses patterns on page 122.)
Long and narrow, this dipper gourd became the future home for a House Wren. The gourd was cleaned and a 1¼" (32mm) hole was cut in the center of the dipper area. Two small holes were drilled in the top of the handle area, of the gourd for a copper wire hanger.

Because dipper gourds are so small in the dipper area they lend themselves more to geometric or whimsical designs than realistic scenes or themes, so I chose a Southwestern design.

Notice in the photos each area is filled with one texture pattern—a scrubbie stroke line, a looped circle pattern, or a fine line fill—yet, each area also has pale, medium, and dark tones.

Use either your temperature setting or how long you keep the tip on the gourd to develop your own graduated fill designs.

Three views of the Southwest Birdhouse gourd.

Close-up photo of Southwest Birdhouse.

Floral Birdhouse

(Uses pattern on page 124.)

The surface of a gourd is inconsistent in density or thickness—you can find very thin areas that will need careful treatment. As you work, you may find areas in the gourd that burn more quickly than other areas or that contain cracks, dents, or discolored areas from where the gourd rested on the ground. These inconsistencies do not detract from your burning work because they only accent that your canvas is a dried gourd. The surface color of a gourd is seldom even; most gourds have dark areas, spots, and even a splotched or speckled coloration.

Supplies:

- 9½" (24cm) diameter, 28" (71cm) circumference kettle gourd
- 12" x 14" (31cm x 36cm) chipboard or heavy cardboard
- Wood glue
- X-Acto or bench knife
- 220-grit sandpaper
- Pyrography system including standard writing tip
- Tracing paper
- #2 soft pencil

1 **Preparing the gourd.** The Floral Birdhouse Project lays flat against the wall for easy display. Begin by cleaning any mold and dirt from the gourds surface. Allow the clean gourd to dry completely, returning to its pale sienna coloring. To create an easy to follow, accurate centerline to cut the gourd into two pieces, fill a sink with about 5" to 6" (13cm to 15cm) of warm water. Carefully lay the gourd into the water on its side so that the stem at the top of the gourd and the blossom end on the bottom side are both partially submerged. Hold the gourd in place for about 1 to 2 minutes. Carefully remove the gourd from the water. You will see a clear, definite water line along the sides of your gourd with one side of the gourd dark from being wet and the other side light-toned from remaining dry. Use a #2 pencil and trace along the water line. Because water is always level, the water line mark left on your gourd is also level and square, giving you a perfect guideline to use to cut the gourd in half.

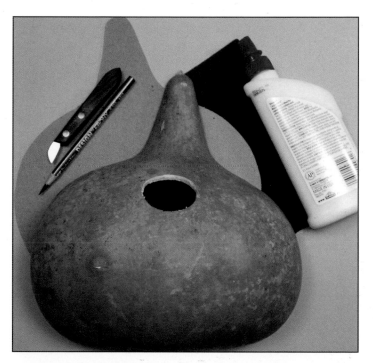

2 **Gather your supplies.** Please wear a dust mask during any cleaning, cutting and scraping steps. Use a gourd saw, X-Acto knife or bench knife to cut your gourd along the pencil guideline. Once you have the gourd cut, remove the seeds and fiber from the inside of the gourd. Soak the gourd half in warm water for several minutes to moisten the inside fibers before your final scraping steps. Allow the gourd to dry completely before you begin your burning steps. Use a spice jar or medicine jar cap as a template and a #2 pencil to mark the birdhouse hole. The hole in my birdhouse is 1¼" (32mm) wide and measures 9" (23cm) from the blossom end of the gourd. Cut this hole using a gourd saw, X-Acto knife, or bench knife. Smooth the cut edges of your gourd with 220-grit sandpaper.

Birdhouse Dimensions:

Bird	Hole Size	Height from Ground
Bluebirds	1½" (38mm)	4'–6' (122cm–183cm)
Carolina Wren	1½" (38mm)	5'–10' (152cm–304cm)
Chickadee	1⅛" (29mm)	6'–15' (183cm–457cm)
Flycatchers	1½" (38mm)	6'–20' (183cm–610cm)
House Finch	1½"(38mm)	5'–15' (152cm–457cm)
House Sparrow	1³⁄₁₆" (30mm)	5'–15' (152cm–457cm)
House Wren	1¼" (32mm)	5'–10' (152cm–304cm)
Nuthatch	1¼" (32mm)	5'–15' (152cm–457cm)
Downy Woodpecker	1¼" (32mm)	5'–15' (152cm–457cm)
Hairy Woodpecker	1½" (38mm)	8'–20' (224cm–610cm)
Purple Martins	1¾" (44mm)	10'–15' (304cm–457cm)
Tree Swallows	1½" (38mm)	5'–15' (152cm–457cm)
Titmouse	1¼" (32mm)	6'–15' (152mm–457cm)
Prothonotary Warble	1⅛" (29mm)	4'–8' (122cm–244cm)
Yellow Bellied Sapsuckers	1½" (38mm)	10'–20' (304cm–610cm)

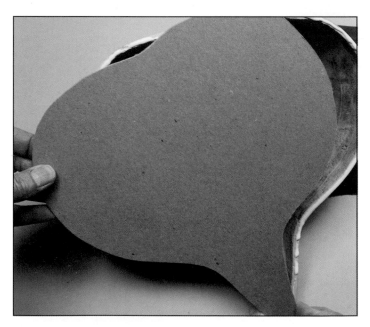

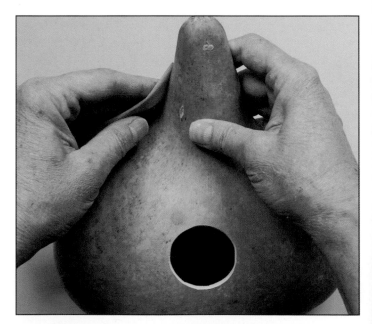

3 **Adding the backboard.** Lay your gourd on a large sheet of chipboard or heavy cardboard. Use a pencil to trace along the outer edge of the gourd. Use an X-Acto knife to cut along the tracing line to create your backing board. Lay a thin bead of wood glue along the edges of the gourd and lay your backing board into place. You can place a book on top of your gourd to add some pressure while the wood glue sets.

4 **Sand the seams.** Using 220 grit sandpaper work along the edges of the chipboard to bring the backing board flush with the sides of the gourd.

5 **Create hanging wire holes.** I used a 12" (31cm) length of 16-gauge copper wire to create a bail wire for hanging. As an alternative you can make a hole in the chipboard back with an X-Acto knife for hanging your gourd.

6 **Pattern challenges.** Because gourds are bowl shaped, tracing a pattern can be difficult. Large flat pieces of paper tend to bend, slide, and buckle on a gourd's curved surfaces. Try cutting your pattern into small, manageable pieces, taping each piece to the gourd. You can also cut darts into the paper pattern that can be folded and taped to make the paper fit the curve of your gourd.

7 **Trace the pattern.** Turn the pattern to the back and rub the back with a #2 to #6 pencil. Tape each pattern piece to your gourd with the pencil rubbed side against the gourd. Allow some overlap. Trace along the outlines of your pattern using an ink pen. Remove the pattern papers from your gourd. Look at your traced pattern and decide which flowers and leaves are foreground elements and which are background elements that tuck under another petal. Use your pencil eraser to remove the excess, overlapped tracing lines from your foreground areas.

8 Black background burn. Because the surface of my gourd is deeply colored, the palest color tones begin in the mid-range. To ensure these mid-range burns will stand out against the natural color of the gourd, I have begun my burning by working the background areas of the patterns with a high-temperature setting between 6 to 7, using a small black touch-and-lift spot pattern with my standard writing tip.

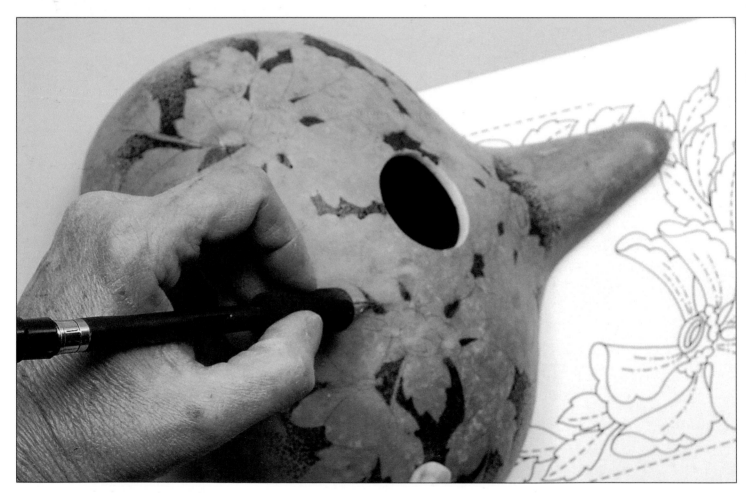

9 Black tones. The closer to the center of the design—the birdhouse hole—the more tightly I have packed the spot pattern. This brings the inside background areas to a solid black tone. Along the outer edges of the pattern, I have worked the spotting pattern along the pattern lines then out into the surrounding background about ½" (13mm). Allow some background around a few leaf points and petals at the outer edges of the pattern to remain unworked, these elements escape beyond the black background. As you work the very outer areas of the background, allow more space between your touch-and-lift spots. To ensure a very black center area to your background, work a second layer of burning with the touch-and-lift spot pattern to the center area of the background.

Note: Gourds come in all shades of brown, from a soft sandy coloring to a coffee with cream tone. How pale a tonal value you can use depends on the gourd's coloring. Light-colored gourds accept pale values where medium-colored gourds may need the burning to start in the mid-range. Adjust your tonal values to the color of your gourd.

10 **Shading petals, leaves, and flower centers.** Shade the design using a medium-temperature setting of 4 to 5, the standard writing tip, and a random scrubbie or random curl stroke. Begin with the flowers' petals. Shade any petal tucked under another petal with the darkest area of the shading at the pattern line of the top petal. Use a random scrubbie stroke to shade where petals connect with the flower center. The petals of these poppies roll over into a U-shape. Shade the rolled petals' underside in a slightly deeper tonal value. Work the deepest part of the shading where the underside of any petal comes into contact and tucks under another element. The undersides of each flower's center need some shading to curve or roll the area. Add a few curved line strokes at the base of each center to separate the centers from the petal areas. Shade the leaves in a deep mid-tone range where any leaf tucks under another leaf or petal. As you work forward, the tips of the leaves lighten the tonal value of your shading. I worked the paler value along the edges of the leaf veins, allowing the veins to remain unburned. Work some light mid-range shading into the wings of the butterfly where the one wing lies under another and where the wings meet the butterfly's body.

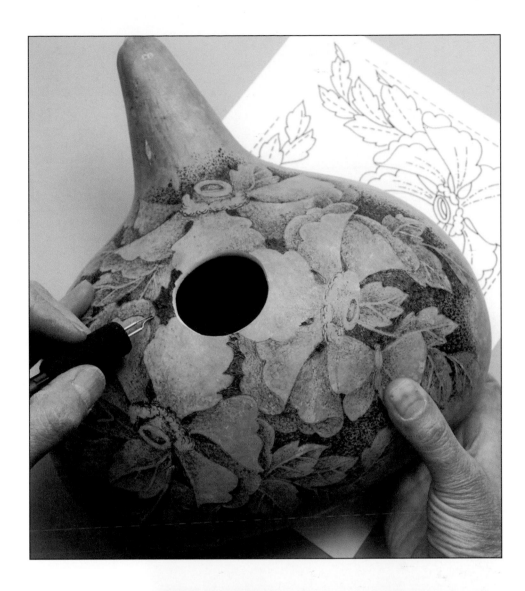

11 **Strengthen petal shading.** Add a second layer of burning to the petals, leaves, and butterfly to darken the shading at the points where one element tucks under another. Work this second layer over one-half or less of the first burning to allow some of the first burning, the areas farthest away from the under-tucks, to remain in their paler tones. You can see in this close-up the darker shades of the second layer of burning. Also notice that the gourd is being sculptured during the burning process. As you burn, the area that you are working is physically lowered into the gourd's surface.

12 Working along the tracing lines. Because you cannot use a wide range of tonal values when working a gourd, your shading work is limited to a few mid-range tones. To ensure your design has a well-defined separation of elements, add a small touch of shading at the tracing lines in the lower element. This step uses a tight random scrubbie stroke to continue the burning texture that has been used throughout the shading steps. This layer of shading is worked as close to the pattern lines as possible. When you are working tight shading strokes, as in this step, have as clean a burning tip as possible to avoid bleeding or scouring into the upper elements.

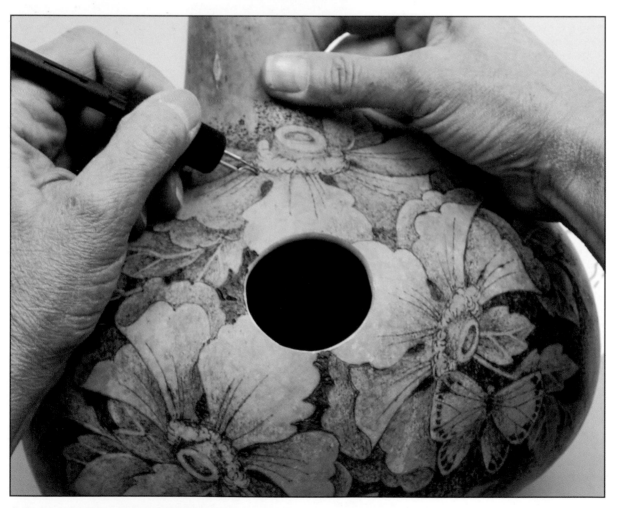

13 Fine detailing. Using a hot temperature setting of 7 and the standard writing tip, add your fine line detailing. Work along the traced pattern lines of the petals where one petal overlaps another or rolls under itself, adding a few long lines to the petals from the center toward the bottom edge of the petal to accent the center of the flower. The butterfly is defined during this step by adding a row of dark spots that becomes the butterfly's body, the veins in the wings and wing markings. Separate the leaves with a detail line where one leaf overlaps another.

Fabric paints

Use fabric paints to hand dye or paint cotton fabrics, creating your own patterns and designs onto the cloth. They offer the benefits of both acrylics and watercolors for the pyrographer. Fabric paints are acrylic-based and become permanent after they have been heat-treated. They do not require a finishing spray sealer to protect the coloring of your project. When working fabrics, the complete painting is ironed to set the color, but a treatment for wood, leather, or gourds in pyrography is to use a hair dryer for several minutes over the surface that has been painted. A spray sealer finish can be applied over fabric paints without any bleeding or distortion of your coloration.

As with watercolors, fabric paints are extremely transparent with no white or gray base added. The palest tonal values of a burning show through fabric paints clearly with no clouding or milky look from the paint layer.

Fabric paints are available in a limited range of colors. True red, bright orange, sun yellow, medium bright green, medium bright blue, and true purple are the basic colors available, along with white and black. They mix easily to create a wider palette of colors and as we work through the coloring steps of the birdhouse you will see some of the possibilities.

Fabric paints for pyrography are thinned with water for use. Use just enough water to be able to read a newspaper through the coloring. Use soft sable brushes for the application of fabric paints.

14 **The completed burn.** Complete the project by adding detail lines. Take time to examine your project and to strengthen any areas that may need a third layer of shading. Gourds may limit the number of distinct tonal values that you can burn into any design but their naturally golden sienna tone and unusual shapes add to a rich feeling to the completed work.

Supplies:

- Fabric paints: yellow, orange, red, green, blue, and white
- Assorted small sable shader and round brushes
- Two pans of clean water—one of mixing and one for brush cleaning
- Glass, ceramic or Styrofoam plate palette
- Paper towels
- Acrylic matte spray sealer
- Hair dryer
- Dried moss, raffia, bamboo skewer sticks
- Hot glue sticks and hot glue gun
- Two small Styrofoam feathered birds
- 12" (31cm) of 16-gauge copper wire
- 4" (102mm) strip of scrap cardboard

1 Applying yellow to the petals. Place a small amount of yellow, about the size of a pea, on a glass or ceramic tile. Use clean water to thin the paint slightly—not quite half and half—with more color than water. Pick up some color on a dampened sable square shader and brush one light coat to the flower petals. Work the color from the flower center toward the petal's edge, until about two-thirds of the petal has been colored. Apply several thin coats instead of one heavy application. Note how transparent and clear fabric paints are and how well the burning tonal values show through the coloration.

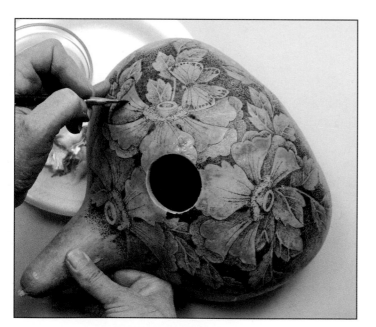

2 Adding orange to the petal edges. Place a small amount of red on your palette. Mix one brush full of yellow with one brush full of red in a separate area of the palette to create orange. Thin with water. The orange mix is painted on the outer edges of the flower petals, adding shading layers over top base coat layers. Use your brush, by working into the yellow areas, to blend the orange and yellow areas into a gradual color change.

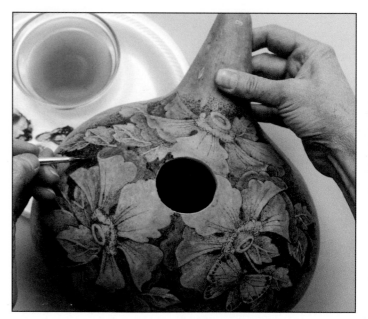

3 Adding red orange. Returning to the orange mixture, add one more brush full of red. This takes the mix into the red-orange color range. This new color is used to paint the underside or rolled-over areas of the petals.

4 **Pale green leaves.** Place a small amount of green on your palette. Mix one brush full of yellow to one brush full of green to create a pale yellow green color. Add water and brush one coat of this new mix on all of the leaves.

5 **Shading colors.** Take a small portion of the orange mixture that you made for step 2, the flower petal edges, and add a small amount of pale green. These two colors—orange and green—mix to become a soft orange brown tone. Thin the color as necessary with water and apply one coat of this orange brown to the flower centers.

6 **Adding white highlights.** Place a small amount of white on your palette and thin with water. White, as with any paint you use in pyrography, is a strong, powerful color. It is better in this step to add a little extra water and use two coats to keep the white pale and transparent. Paint the thinned white on the fiber base area of the flower center.

7 **Intense color spots.** A small brush stroke of bright orange has been applied to one side of the flower center over the orange brown coloring. This is just a small accent to brighten and strength this area.

8 **Petal highlights.** Add a small amount of yellow to the thinned white to create a pale yellow color. Use one or two brush strokes of the mix along the long detail lines in the petals.

9 **Multiple shading layers.** Mix one brush full of yellow with one brush full of your orange mixture to create a yellow-orange color. A small brush stroke of yellow-orange has been worked on the top layers of the petals where one petal tucks under another petal.

10 **Adding dark green shading.** Place a small amount of blue on your palette. Mix one brush full of green with one brush full of blue to create a deep green color. Add more green if necessary to keep the mix away from the blue-green range. Thin this mix with water and add a few brush strokes of shading to the leaves where one leaf tucks under another leaf.

11 **Adding spray sealer.** When the painting steps are completed, allow your gourd to dry thoroughly—at least one hour. You can set your fabric color by using a hair dryer set on high. Work the hot air over the surface of the gourd for several minutes or until the gourd feels evenly warm across it's surface. I finished my gourd using an acrylic matte spray sealer. Follow the directions on the can and use the spray sealer outdoors or in a very well ventilated area. Use two to three light coats. Allow the sealer to dry thoroughly.

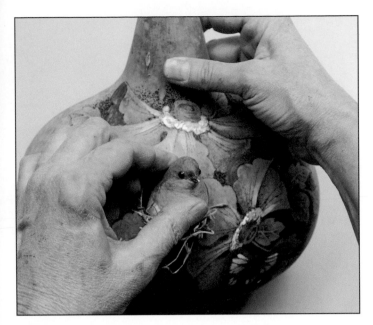

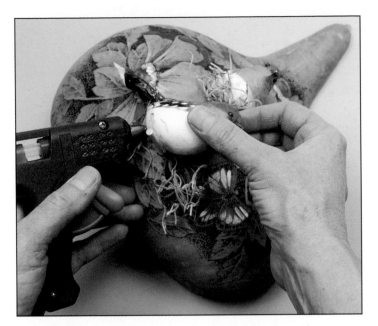

12 **Adding fun accents.** I gathered some dried moss, raffia, a bamboo kitchen skewer, my hot glue gun, and two Styrofoam feathered birds. Using a hot glue gun, glue a small amount of dried moss the lower edge of the birdhouse hole. Let some of the moss escape beyond the hole's opening. Apply hot glue to the bottom of one of your feathered birds. Place this bird in the hole with about one-half of its body extended out from the hole. Hold the bird in place until the hot glue cools.

13 **Adding the perch.** Using your X-Acto knife or bench knife, cut a 2" (51mm) length of wood from a bamboo kitchen skewer. Approximately 2" to 2½" (51mm to 64mm) below the birdhouse hole, make a smaller hole to accept the skewer perch. Hot glue the skewer perch into position. Place a small amount, several strands, of dried moss on top of the skewer perch and hot glue these to the birdhouse. Apply hot glue to the bottom of your second feathered bird and attach him to the skewer perch. Add a second drop of hot glue to the bird's back where it will touch the walls of the birdhouse. Hold this bird in place until the hot glue cools.

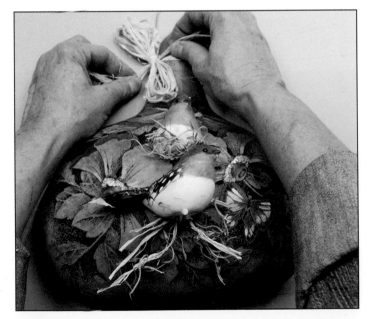

14 **Raffia accents.** Cut a strand of raffia into several 3" to 4" (76mm to 102mm) lengths. Fold each piece in half and add a drop of hot glue at the fold point. Add the raffia accents to the birdhouse hole and to the perch area. Make two small holes with your bench knife in the top handle area of the gourd to receive the bent ends of the copper wire. Set the copper wire in place and secure with hot glue. Add a raffia bow and your birdhouse is complete and ready to display.

Whimsical Farm Scene Birdhouse

(Uses pattern on page 123.)

Wraparound scenes. Gourds are perfect for wrap around scenes. Some patterns deserve lots of careful, graduated shading worked with a medium-wide or spoon-shaped shader. Other patterns deserve a range of tonal values and extremely fine detailing. The Whimsical Farm Scene Birdhouse pattern is just a fun, primitive design using medium-toned outlining and a few texture strokes as small looping circles and scrubbie strokes.

Fill spaces in. Transfer each pattern on the gourd then fill in the spaces between the patterns with small pine trees or fields. After cleaning, I cut a 1¼" (32mm) hole in the front for the house entry portal. A scrap of gourd left from the Pine Cone Bird Feeder was cut to become a porch roof and glued into place using hot glue. Watercolor paints and gloss acrylic spray sealer complete the burned project. The original stem of the gourd makes the perch and then use 12-gauge wire for the hanger. This project makes a fun, fast decoration for your garden.

Posies Cachepot

(Uses pattern on page 124.)

Posies Cachepot. By simply changing the pattern to this Posies design and following the step-by-step instructions for the Floral Birdhouse Gourd on page 48 you can create a bright, decorative cachepot for your African violets. This project uses heavy, dark tonal values behind the flower pattern to separate the design area of the gourd from the unworked area below the flowers.

Practice board. Some practice boards focus on the surface being used; this one focuses on developing the design. My test burning for this pattern was worked on 6" (91cm) square of white chipboard using a variable-temperature unit and my standard writing and spoon shader tip pens. I wanted to keep the background petals in a mid-tone range and avoid using black tones with the flower. The mid-tone range of pyrography is about the same tonal value as the natural, unburned surface of the gourd. To separate the two areas—the mid-tone petals from the mid-tone gourd—I chose a dark, black-brown burning to surround the flower design.

Pinecone Bird Feeder

(Uses pattern on page 125.)

Pinecone Bird Feeder. Transform this canteen gourd into a winter bird feeder by cutting an extra large hole in the gourd on the stem side. This hole measures 4½" (11cm) on a 9" (23cm) diameter gourd. Using a medium to hot temperature setting and the standard writing tip, the pattern was first outlined following the tracing lines. Because this particular gourd has a very rough, sandy texture to its surface, the outline appears as a broken textured line. That same texture effect was carried into the rest of the pattern with dark touch-and-lift dot texture in the deep areas of the pinecone petals and then accented with fine line work in the forward section of each petal. The leaves are shaded with fine line work coming from the center vein line toward the leaf edge. Tightly packed scrubbie strokes shade the grapevine wreath. Fabric paints and gloss acrylic spray sealer finish the surface of the gourd. Two small holes were cut just below the opening and a cinnamon stick was added using cotton crochet thread worked through the holes and over the stick perch.

Native American Bead Rattle

(Uses pattern on page 126.)

My practice board for learning to work gourds began with this dipper gourd that measures 14" high by 15" (36cm by 38cm) in circumference. The upper portion had a clean, smooth surface but the lower half was deeply crackled. So only one half of the gourd was worthy of burning. A simple solution to was to create a wire beaded cage around the lower half of the gourd, hiding the crackling, while turning this gourd into a Native American-styled rattle.

1 **Wash the gourd.** Clean the gourd in warm water and soap.

2 **Empty the gourd.** Cut a 1" to 1½" (25mm to 38mm) diameter hole in the bottom (blossom end) of the gourd. Remove seeds and core.

3 **The pattern.** Trace the pattern for the Native American Rattle Gourd, repeating one of the scroll curves around the centerline at one-half the total height of your gourd. Extend the pointed spikes of the pattern to the base of the stem.

4 **Outlines.** Using the standard writing tip and a medium temperature setting, outline each of the pattern lines.

5 **Textures and patterns.** Fill in the space captured between the spiked arms using different texture and stroke patterns. Small, tightly packed repetitive patterns worked best for my gourd.

6 **Black tonal value.** Fill the small circles of the design with a touch-and-lift dot pattern on a high setting until the spots become a black tonal value.

7 **Wire netting pattern.** Cut a 15" (38cm) length of 12-gauge copper wire, a soft and easy to manipulate wire. Hold the wire against a large vitamin jar—about 3" (76mm) in diameter—and roll the wire around the jar's sides to create a large circle. Allow a little wire on each end of the circle. Bend both ends of the 12-gauge wire around your bent-nose pliers into small loops. Open one and loop with your pliers, thread it inside the other loop, then close that loop to lock your circle together.

You can bead-wrap the wire circle using long lengths of 26-gauge wire and 6mm beads. Wrap the 26-gauge wire 6 to 10 times around the 12-gauge wire, add a 6mm bead, create a second wrap of 6 to 10 turns of the fine wire. Continue wrapping and adding beads until the entire circle is covered. To secure the ends of this fine wire, crimp the ends tightly against the 12-gauge wire using flat-nose pliers.

8 **Wire bead cage.** To create the wire bead cage, cut one 36" (91cm) length of 26-gauge wire for every two wire wrapped beads that you used to cover the large circle. Attach the wires to the large circle by folding the wire in half and using a half-hitch over the large circle. Place one new 26-gauge half-hitched wire between every two large circle beads. Make a half-hitch by placing the loop of the fold in front of the circle wire. Take the two ends of the wire behind the large circle then thread them through the loop. Pull the two ends to tighten the loop. On my gourd, I have 28 6mm beads that covered the large circle and 16 to 26 half-hitched wires.

Supplies:

- Dipper gourd 4" high x 15" (10cm x 38cm) circumference.
- 12-gauge copper wire
- 26-gauge copper wire
- One 15" (38cm) strand of 8mm glass beads
- Two 15" (38cm) strands of 6mm glass beads
- 12" (31cm) leather cord
- Leather scraps
- Pheasant feathers
- Paint brush with a small, thin handle
- Flat-nose pliers
- Bent-nose pliers
- Wire cutters

Wire netting pattern.

Wire ending.

9 **Fish net pattern.** The beads of the rattle are added to the wire in a fishnet pattern. Take one wire from one half-hitch knot, add one 6mm bead to the wire. Take one wire from the adjacent half-hitch wire and add one 6mm bead to this wire. Hold the two wires together and thread them through one 8mm bead. Knot the pair of wires until you have completed one row. Repeat for each half-hitch.

10 **Wire ending.** As you work the netting, allow about ½" (13mm) of wire between each 8mm bead. To hold the 8mm bead in place as you work the remaining row, fold the two wires at the base of the bead into a right angle to the bead—one wire in one direction and the second wire in the opposite direction. This holds the bead while placing the wires in position for the next row. I found it easiest to work the netting in place over my gourd with the gourd held upside down. Keep the netting loose around the gourd; you want the beaded cage to have lots of room to move. Continue making rows of beaded netting until the netting measures 1" (25mm) longer than the base of the gourd.

11 **Tying the wires.** At the base of the last bead on each row, tie a simple overhand knot using both wires held together.

12 **Centering wires.** Pick up the knotted bead wires in one hand. Center the wires over the cut hole in the bottom of the gourd. Tie the bundle of wires into a simple overhand knot. If your wires are too short for this step, use a 6" (15cm) piece of 26-gauge wire and wrap it around the bead wires to secure them together. Working one wire at a time, hold one wire against the handle of a small paintbrush. Wrap the wire around that handle to create a tightly packed coil. Coil each of the wires. You can add a bead to these end wires before you coil them.

13 **Sound.** Add feathers, beads, shells, and scrap leather to the large circle of the netting for the final decoration. Now, shake the rattle—the loose-netted beads make a wonderful "chink" sound when they strike your gourd.

Chipboard

Chipboard is an excellent substrate offering several unique features for the artist. Available in a range of colors from soft beige-orange to solid dark gray, chipboard starts your work in a mid-tone value range much like the old sepia photos common in the late-1800s. Dark tonal burnings become crisp black colorings against the chipboard background. Mid-tone values develop quickly with only a few layers of texture.

Because it is used primarily as a packing material, chipboard is available in extremely large sizes, either through an office supply store or at a packaging company. The thickness of chipboard varies from ⅛" to ¼" (3mm to 6mm).

The cost of purchasing chipboard can be minimal. If you take some time to look around your house you may have several pieces available for your use. For smaller projects, consider using the back of a stenographer's pad, spiral school notebook, and even the inside of a cereal box. Check any shipping boxes that have arrived as often a sheet of chipboard is used to line the bottom of packing boxes.

Chipboard can easily be cut using a craft or bench knife and with scrapbook hole punches. The thickness of the board prevents cupping or curling during the burning process.

The medium brown-gray coloring is perfect for colored pencil work, making the pale pencil colors as white, light yellow, and orange stand out boldly against the darker burned areas. Chipboard coated with white paper is also available through scrapbook supply stores, providing the same easy-to-work surface with pure white coloring as your background.

Completed Steampunk Photo Frame.

Steampunk Photo Frame

(Uses pattern on page 128.)

Supplies:

- Variable-temperature pyrography system
- Standard writing tip pen
- Flat spoon shade tip pen
- Wide shaper tip pen
- Graphite paper for pattern tracing
- For tracing: compass, metal ruler, right angle triangle
- 12" x 12³⁄₁₆" x ⅛" (31cm x 31.5cm to 3mm) piece of chipboard
- Leather strop or emery cloth for tool tip cleaning
- Coloring and photo supplies
- Three to four computer reproduced photos
- Transparent tape
- Craft utility knife or bench knife
- Assortment of 12 artist-quality watercolor pencils
- Spray sealer—Reworkable Fixatif
- 12" x 12" (31cm x 31cm) shadow box frame.

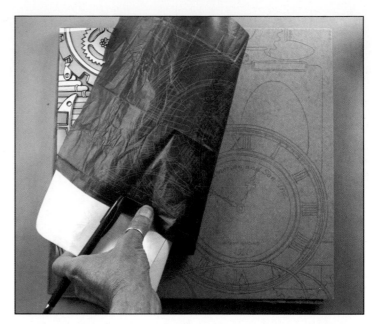

1 Tracing the pattern. Resize the pattern to 12" square. Cut your chipboard to measure 12" x 12" (31cm x 31cm). A craft utility knife or bench knife and a metal ruler will do the job. Center the pattern over your chipboard and use a small strip of transparent tape to secure the top edge of the pattern to the top edge of the chipboard. Slide a sheet of graphite paper between the pattern and chipboard. Using an ink pen, trace along the pattern outlines.

2 Create a practice board. Cut a scrap piece of chipboard to use as a practice board. Work a sample burning with each of the three pen tips that will be used here—the standard writing tip, the spoon shader tip, and a flat or wide shader tip. Begin each sample area using a low-temperature setting and a simple crosshatch pattern. Continue working small crosshatch patterns each time turning the temperature setting slightly higher. For my practice board, I used a pencil to mark which pen tip and what temperature setting I used for each crosshatch pattern. I use the practice board as a reference guide while I work the project.

Chipboard Practice Board

(Uses pattern on page 127.)

Chipboard is easy to cut with an X-Acto or bench knife and lends itself to creating cut-out holiday decorations. These hanging ornaments measure 6" (152mm) high and were worked using the backing chipboard from a student's spiral notebook.

The Santa, Santa Bear, and Elf patterns were traced onto the chipboard notebook back using graphite paper and then cut with a bench knife. Make two of each pattern piece.

The burning was worked using the standard writing tip pen. Watercolor pencils were used to give each ornament their bright coloring. Work both cut pieces—one for the front of your ornament and one for the back.

Use two 3" (76mm) pieces of heavy cotton twine for each ornament. Hot glue the twine legs to the back of one of the burned figures. Hot glue the duplicate cut chipboard figure to the back, covering the twine and making the ornaments reversible.

Completed pyrography stage of ornaments.

Santa Claus and Santa Bear.

3 **Cut the photo frame holes.** Using a bench knife or craft utility knife cut the chipboard along the pattern lines to open the frame areas. Using your standard writing tip pen and a medium-high temperature setting, roll the pen tip along the inside edge of the cut lines to create a dark tone burning and to smooth the cut edges.

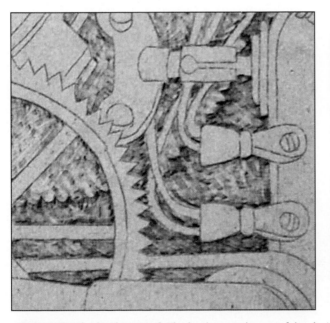

4 **Burning the background.** The background areas of the design have been worked in a small pull stroke texture using the wide edge of a flat shader and a medium temperature setting of 6. This creates a mottled uneven pattern throughout the background of the design. Still using the flat shader and a heat setting of 6, the background is darkened where the main pattern gears, arms and clock face would cast a shadow onto the background area. For this design, the light source is assumed to be coming from the upper left-hand side of the design. This places the background-cast shadows on the lower right side of the main pattern elements.

5 Working the electric transformer.
Using the standard writing tip and a medium, 5 to 6, temperature setting create a crosshatch shading to the lower one third of the electric transformer. Several graduated layers of shading will create a rolled or curved feeling to this element. Work the crosshatching along the outer edges of the transformer. Using a simple, tightly packed line texture, work the sides of the transformer plate to a medium dark tone. Outline along the three electric wires and work a small amount of crosshatch shading onto the transformer on the right-hand side of each wire. The screw and rivet are outlined and then the transformer is shaded using a crosshatch stroke on the right side of the both. Take the crosshatch shading into the bottom half of the pipe or conduit that runs through the transformer and behind the clock. Work crosshatch pattern in several layers to create the curve of the pipe. Outline and shade the three rings on the conduit pipe.

6 Working the electrical connectors. The electrical connectors are first outlined using the standard writing tip and a medium-high temperature to make a dark clean line. Shade the connectors behind the screw areas with crosshatching and outline the screw heads. Add shading to the electric cords where they tuck under another element using either tightly packed fine lines or crosshatching. You can deepen the cast shadows that the cords create on the background by working over the pull strokes of the flat shader with a tight scrubbie stroke using the standard writing tip. A fine line design is burned onto the transformer to create an engraving pattern. This is done at a medium-high temperature setting and using the writing tip.

7 **Shading the upper background gear.** For the upper background gear use a wide flat shader and a long pull stroke to begin the tonal value work. Follow this overall shading with the crosshatch texturing. Re-enforce the background if necessary to deepen the shadows behind this upper gear. Below the upper background gear is a set of graduated pipes. Using the standard writing tip and a short fine line shade the lower half of each pipe worked on the diagonal to the first lines. Repeat this shading in the lower one-fourth area of each pipe. Outline the three bands on the pipes using the standard writing tip. Work the electrical connector at the top of the pipes in a manner similar to the ones near the transformer. The metal plate that lies over the pipes is another excellent area to personalize the design. A name, date, or location could be added or, as in this sample, a small engraving design. Shade the pipes on the right-hand side of the metal plate to cast a shadow from the plate using the wide flat shader. Because there are no elements that will cast a shadow on this arm, an engraving design, personalization, or both, can be used to decorate this area.

8 **Shading the lower background gear.** The background gear above the transformer is shaded with a tight crosshatch texture. The closer the gear teeth lie to another element, as the armature above the gear, the more layers of crosshatching are used to darken the tonal value. I have added a name—The Acme Gear Company—in a script lettering to the wide section of this gear. You can personalize the name that you choose so that it reflects something about the person whose photos will be in the frame. The area of this background gear that lies above and behind the armature is the darkest value of the gear.

9 **Adding fine details and personalizing.** The armature is a long area that lies in the foreground of the design. The armature above is accented with a complimentary engraving design. Detail the upper armature gear using the standard writing tip. In the close-up image, you can see the crosshatch texturing that shades both armatures. Looking to the right side of this image, the shading falls onto the armatures where the clock face covers them. The top armature has two metal areas behind the arm, one that goes behind the top gear. These areas are the darkest tonal value in this step.

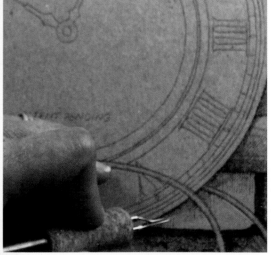

10 **Working the lower right corner of the photo frame.** There are three electrical connectors and one skate key in the upper right quadrant of the design. These are shaded using both the wide flat shader with a layering of crosshatching done with the standard writing tip. While working this area, I also darkened the original background toning to enhance the electrical connectors. Crosshatch shading with the standard writing tip accents the photo frame. The metal plate at the top of the frame holds my Dad's birth and death years. A fine line engraving completes this section. The photo frame extends below the clock face and is shaded with the same crosshatch texturing as the rest of the frame.

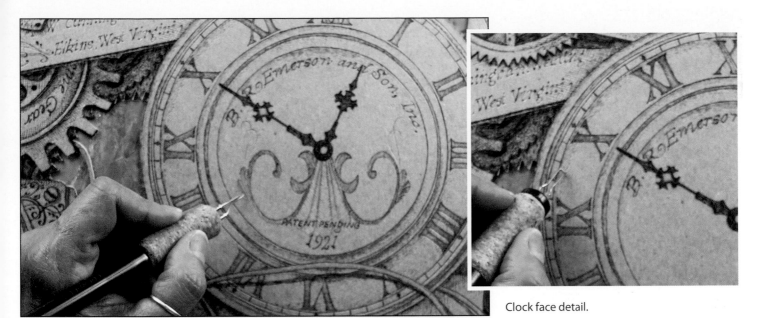

Clock face detail.

11 Clock Face. The numerals of the clock face were outlined using the standard writing tip and a medium-temperature setting and then filled with a crosshatch texture. The circles and minute marks also used a medium temperature with the standard writing tip. The clock hands have been filled with a touch-and-lift dot pattern to create a very dark tone. Personalize the clock using a manufacturer's name and date that reflect the person in the photos. The inner circles at the top right and bottom left use a medium-temperature setting and a random doodle or scrubbie stroke. This simple gives the clock face a little more tonal value work. A pale-toned lower-center design adds a little more decoration. This was worked using fine lines that all flow in the same direction.

12 Burning complete. The completed burning has the look of an old photograph. Chipboard requires no finishing products—sprays or sealers.

Adding Color

1 **Watercolor colored pencils.** Start the coloring using white pencil to create bright highlight areas throughout the design. You can see these highlights in the spiral gear top left, the adjacent round gear top left, the two armatures, the metal plate on the transformer, the upper edge of the transformer pipe, and in the clock face. This photo shows about three layers of color work. Cadmium yellow was used next to accent the areas just worked in white. Peach adds coloring the some of the mid-ground gears. Light turquoise shades the transformer pipe, the inside areas of the upper left spiral gear, and the inner circles on the clock face.

2 Adding more colors. As you work your coloring use a small amount of each color in all four quadrants of the design. A touch of olive green is used on the metal plate that attaches to the armatures. Also use olive green on the transformer pipe, in one of the lower left clock circles, and in the upper photo frame near the electrical connectors.

3 Layers intensify colors. Adding layers of color add intensity. Working the entire design again, new highlights have been added using white. Orange tones have been worked in the background layer of burning and red has been worked throughout the upper level foreground of the design. Pale to medium green and red have added color to the electric wires.

4 Creating extra gears. Because my frame is a shadow box frame with about 1" (25mm) of space between the glass and the completed photo burning, I have room to make extra gears to fill in the shadow box space. I have created a few extra gear patterns to chipboard, cut them out using my bench knife, and then burned the detail just as we worked the gears in the photo frame. Because the gears will sit in front of the photo frame, I have added color pencil work. These gears have several more layers of coloring to make them more intense than the photo frame gears. A touch of clear water on a soft bristle brush blends the watercolor pencils.

5 Adding the photos. Make copies of your family photos to use behind the Steam Punk Clock Frame. These are held in place on the back of the chipboard using transparent tape. The extra gears can be added along the edges using white glue or a hot glue gun.

Daylily Cork Board

(Uses pattern on page 130.)

Cork-Framed Daylily design on white chipboard—a perfect cheery place to post notes.

White chipboard offers the same ease of use in pyrography as the natural sepia toned surface with the bright whiteness allowing for pale tonal value work and watercolor or colored pencil application.

This daylily was worked on an 8" by 8" white chipboard. The pale burnings can be seen in the lower left hand petal of the flower. Small accents of color—bright yellow, hot pink, and medium green—were added after burning was complete.

To matte this project, I cut two pieces of scrapbooking paper that matched the hot pink tones in the flower. The pink paper was cut at 9½" (24cm) and the mauve purple at 9" (23cm).

Each paper was layered as shown onto a 12" (31cm) square of corkboard and glued into place using contact cement.

Daylily on white chipboard.

Papier-Mâché

Papier-mâché is a favorite pyrography surface for me. Made from shredded craft paper and glue, the papier-mâché can be pressed into a variety of shapes from flower pots, kitchen canisters, gift boxes, and even scrap book covers. It is inexpensive and requires no preparation steps.

The medium-to-brown gray coloring is perfect for either colored pencil or pastel chalk application over your burning.

Texture patterns. A few simple texture patterns are needed to complete the Sunflower Yarn Box Pattern. The three samples shown are all dot textures useful for filling an area or to add shading. When using a one-temperature solid tip pen, the depth of the shading is controlled by the amount of time that the pen tip touches the surface.

Papier-mâché is made of the same compressed fibers as chipboard but comes in a large selection of fun pre-formed shapes. Just about any shape you can imagine is available, from small comical piggy banks to nesting boxes and holiday decorations.

Papier-Mâché Notes:

- Up to a ¼" (6mm)-thick papier-mâché pre-made shapes provide a firm, strong working surface. However, because this is shredded paper, the pen tip will leave an indented impression on the top layer. In the upper right hand corner of the photo sample, you can see that some of the small circles are dropped down into the surface.

- The small pieces of papier-mâché used to create shapes are uneven in thickness. That means the working surface does not have a uniform density. Some areas will burn quickly while others seem to resist the burn. Notice on the center right of the photo there are some small circles that are almost black while the circles around those are barely toned.

- Avoid using graphite or carbon paper on papier-mâché—they become embedded in the indentations that can be made by the tracing pen. Instead use a pencil rub on the back of your pattern. After the burning is complete use an artist's eraser to remove any remaining pattern lines.

Indentations. Because papier-mâché has a firm structure but soft surface, your burning will leave indentations. When completed, your project will not only have tonal value but also actual depth and physical texture. This is a close-up of the Grocery Bag Practice Board. (See page 23 for the full-sized Grocery Bag Practice Board.)

Coloring Suggestions:

Paints, such as watercolors or acrylics, can damage your papier-mâché burning because they soak into the upper surface.

Try artist-quality colored pencils as your coloring media. Using a sharp pencil and thin layers of application will add bright color tones without losing the tonal value of the pyro work.

Because this surface comes in a mid-tone beige, pale colored pencils add bright, light areas to your design.

Close-up. Colored pencil work on papier-mâché.

Sunflower Yarn Caddy

(Uses pattern on page 131.)

For this project, I used a pre-formed papier-mâché yarn caddy box. Papier-mâché is a product created by mixing finely shredded paper scraps with a white glue-based media. This makes the papier-mâché easy to shape and very firm in consistency—a great burning surface.

The design is a wraparound sunflower pattern with a butterfly placed across one of the side edges of the box. When the woodburning steps were complete, I used artist-quality colored pencils to add the bright vivid yellows, red browns, and oranges to the flower's petals with green and blue tones for my butterfly. The background, unburned area of the box was toned with dark blue, purple, and grey tones to set the flower colors forward. The outside of the papier-mâché box was sealed with several light coats of polyurethane spray.

To finish this project, I made a simple cloth bag to place inside my box so that my sunflower caddy can be used as a dried flower holder, yarn needle box, or for tall kitchen matches near the fireplace.

Completed pyrography stage.

1 Getting started. Rub the back of your pattern with a soft #2 to #6 pencil. Place the pattern paper against your wine caddy with the bottom edge of your pattern in line with the bottom edge of your papier-mâché caddy. Trace along your pattern lines using an ink pen.

2 Pyrography tools. Burn this project using both the standard writing and shader tips on a variable-temperature unit. Develop the tonal values slowly using a random doodle texture, line texture, and dot pattern.

First layer of colored pencil work.

3 **Continuous pattern.** Burn this design as one continuous pattern, going right around the corners on the petals, center, and butterfly, while keeping your tonal values even. Leave the highlight areas inside of the sunflower petals, center, and butterfly unburned.

4 **First layer of colored pencil work.** Because the colors are transparent, you can lay one color over another to create new color hues. Develop your pencil work in light, thin layers of color. The first several color layers are barely visible. It is not until your reach the fourth or fifth layer that you will begin seeing the color over each area. A colored pencil work can easily have twenty or more layers of color. Stick color pencils are often used for large area application because of their thickness. A few selected background colors make a great addition to your color pencil set. Keep your pencils extremely sharp. This helps to keep the pencil work on the high, unburned, or lightly burned areas of your design.

5 **Second layer of colored pencil work.** Artist-quality colored pencils are perfect for adding bright yellows, oranges, and red browns to this project. There are several grades of colored pencils available for the pyrographers, including artist-quality color pencils, watercolor pencils, and color pencil sticks. Artist-quality colored pencils use a wax base for the color pigment, which, when properly applied, keeps the colors transparent. The transparency allows the tonal values of your pyrography to show through the color work.

6 **Final layer of pencils and spray sealer coat.** Note how transparent colored pencils are—you can clearly see all of the wood burning work right through the vibrant coloring. The completed pencil color has approximately twenty layers of color added. Once the pencil work is completed you will want to seal the outside surface of your wine caddy with several light layers of polyurethane or acrylic spray sealer. Because the substrate of papier-mâché is a white glue-based media, your spray sealer can have a splotchy cloudy appearance when first applied. After the piece has been allowed to dry thoroughly, at least one half hour per coat, that splotchy effect will disappear to a crystal clear finish.

Artist Paper

Artists use many styles of paper working in watercolors, illustration markers, pastels, and hand-pulled prints. The same heavyweight, fine-quality papers are suitable for pyrography. The poundage of art papers is measured by the weight of 500 sheets of 17" by 22" (43cm x 56cm) sheets. So 140-pound paper means 500 17" by 22" inch sheets of that particular paper weights 140 pounds. The heavier the paper's weight; thicker the paper.

Rag content artist paper come in several textures. You can find papers ranging from a very smooth light textured surface to a deep pebbled texturing. For pyrography, a smooth or light texture works well. Papers with pebbled or other heavily textured surfaces can distort your lines as you burn.

Artist Paper Notes:

- Of all of the burning surfaces available to pyrographers, paper is perhaps the hardest media to work. Even though it is a wood pulp product, the addition of bleach, softeners, and glue add to the paper's resistance to cool temperature-setting strokes.

- As you work any paper surface, be patient. The early stages of shading help to break down the additives, making later layers develop more quickly.

Art papers come not only in individual sheets but also as rolls, pads, and even pre-made envelopes and letter writing papers.

Practice Design

Paper burning often has a limited number of tonal values with few pale tones and almost no black tones because it requires a higher heat setting before any burning strokes show. To expand your value range try using strong bold textures and varying degrees of detail work to create your very palest and darkest values.

There are several types of paper surfaces from which you can chose. Any paper made from natural ingredients can be used for pyrography, but avoid papers that have plastic or glitter accents added, such as some scrapbooking and gift wrapping papers. Also avoid papers that have a shiny, polished finish to their surface.

Thin or lightweight papers can buckle from the uneven distribution of heat during the burning process. So a lightweight typing or computer print paper will not remain flat. Heavier papers, such as card stock, illustration board, and watercolor paper, easily accept burning with little or no distortion.

Artist paper can be colored using watercolors, watercolor pencils, and artist pastels. In this sample watercolor pencils are being applied. After several thin coats of both a base and shading colors, a soft bristle brush dampened with water allows the pencils to be smoothed and blended.

Paper Dragon—a practice design for artist paper. (Uses pattern on page 133.)

Protecting your paper. Any paper surface will grab dirt and oil from your hands as you work. Use a sheet of transparent velum larger than the project paper and cut a window in the velum that is slightly larger than the design to cover the working paper and protect it as the project develops.

Home Sweet Home Paper Burning

(Uses pattern on page 132.)

Watercolor paper or illustration board with some rag content will burn at a slightly lower temperature than those without. The small amount of cotton fibers in rag content papers means it will be easier to develop pale tones.

Artist papers come in a range of surface textures and colors. The sample shown here is worked on a smooth cream-colored paper. You can also find pure white, ivory, fawn, beige, chocolate, and black papers. The color of the paper will affect how well your burning work shows. A dark chocolate paper may show only the very darkest of burning tones, a fawn paper will show both the dark and mid-tone values, and a white or cream paper will allow for pale mid-tones.

While paper does have the disadvantages of needing a very hot temperature setting and having a limited tonal range, it does have several outstanding assets as a pyrography medium. Learning to work paper allows you to create greeting cards and matching envelopes, to accent the matting that surrounds your framed woodburning, and to incorporate the wonderful bits of flowers, leaves, and color found in handmade papers into your design. Paper is a widely available product that can be inexpensively purchased at any art and crafts store. After completing the burning, add color using watercolors, acrylics, or colored pencil, with little or no color distortion caused by beige and tan wood or leather.

Home Sweet Home has very little spoon shader work. Instead, it depends on fine line burning strokes to develop both the shading effects and the detailing. Begin the project by taping the outer edges of the watercolor paper to the drawing board. Taping reduces the paper's natural tendency to buckle or warp during burning. To transfer the pattern, rub the back of the pattern paper with a soft pencil (numbers 2 to 6) lay the rubbed side against the watercolor paper, and trace the pattern lines using an ink pen.

Using graphite or carbon paper to transfer patterns onto your working paper is not advised—on paper both can become permanent, especially if the hot pyrography pen touches the actual tracing line. That can leave you with a very black detail line from the carbon with the rest of the burning. While there was no carbon in the mid-dark range. By using a pencil rubbing, I know that when the burning is completed, any extra tracing lines will erase easily and completely.

1 **Pale tonal value.** Through the first mapping stage, use a standard writing tip at a setting between 6 to 7 and a simple short line stroke to establish the shading in the trees, bushes, and under the roof lines in the house. Work the pine trees and stone walk in the same short line stroke with a slightly hotter setting. This first burning was done mostly to begin breaking down the glues and additives in the paper in preparation for the hotter burns in layer two and three.

Supplies:

- 140 lb. or heavier cold press watercolor paper, 12" x 12" (31cm x 31cm)
- Pyrography system with standard writing tip and large spoon shader

2 Adding medium tones. Having established where to shade, the second burning layer concentrates on areas where the darkest tonal values were needed. Paper does not accept layers of burning the way that wood, leather, and gourds do. Instead of working an area with multiple burning layers to achieve a black tone on paper, it often is better to simply turn up the temperature setting. This dark value work was done at a setting near 8 with a red-hot tip. Watercolor pads or blocks are perfect to use. The paper, up to 22" by 30" (56cm by 76cm), is stacked then glued along the four outer edges, making the stack into one strong board. As you work, the paper cannot buckle because of the heat of the pen. When the burning is finished, the top paper you have worked is cut free from the block and the next paper on the block is ready to use. You can also find in watercolor rag content paper pre-cut greeting cards and envelopes that make wonderful presents.

3 Third layer—blacks and detailing. The last burning stage for Home Sweet Home added the fine detailing in the inside of the tree leaf clusters, along the outer edge of those clusters as well as the detailing for the house, shrubs, and the hanging tire swing. The lettering was done is a random curl and scrubbie stroke to make that area as dark as possible. Because it is created from finely shredded wood and cotton fibers, paper does not burn as evenly as other pyro surfaces. Sudden changes in tonal value are common and add to the dynamics of an artist paper burn.

Cotton Fabric and Canvas

Add cotton canvas items such as totes, book bags, and aprons to your list of ideas for your next pyrography project. Fabric burning can create tonal values from very pale soft browns to rich dark russet tones. Any cotton fabric can be used for pyrography, but the thickness of canvas weave makes it the ideal fabric. Also consider working a burned design on pale-colored all-cotton blue jeans, a white all-cotton denim jacket, an all-cotton T-shirt, or an all-cotton canvas tote bag. All-cotton fibers burn evenly and beautifully.

Pre-wash fabric first to remove any sizing or starch. Blot off excess water with a thick towel so your project is slightly damp. Stretch the damp fabric out over several layers of cardboard, pinning it in place with long quilting pins. When the fabric has dried completely, it will have pulled taut to the cardboard, making it easy to work.

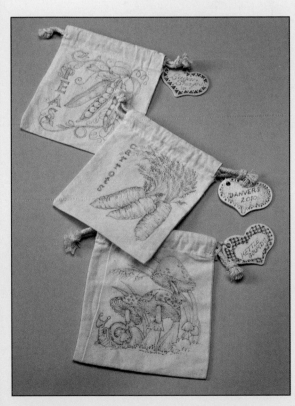

No damage. As a practice board project for cloth, use untreated cotton muslin or canvas to evenly burn a nice range of pale to medium russet tones without damaging the fabric. The designs above were worked on lightweight unbleached muslin wedding favor bags using Carrot, Peas, Pumpkin, Mushroom, and Butterfly patterns. (Uses patterns on pages 135–137.)

Make-up bag. Valentine Girl Make-Up Bag burned on cotton canvas bag with pink fabric paint accents. A small burned wooden zipper tag completes the project. (Uses pattern on page 134.)

Notes for cotton fabric:

- Fabric comes in a variety of weights from very thin, lightweight T-shirts to heavyweight cottons. Each weight burns best at a slightly different temperature setting.

- To begin a project without practicing on similar fabric first, start burning at a low temperature setting. Try a few strokes, then if needed raise the temperature setting slightly. Slowly bring your pen tip up to the desired heat.

- Keep your pen tip moving, with a slow steady pace, at all times. Allowing the pen to touch and rest on the fabric can burn through the fibers and create a small hole.

- For very dark burns, use multiple layers of your medium-to-hot settings, slowly darkening the area.

- If your clothing item is heavily starched from the manufacturing process, wash the item first in warm water. Allow the cloth to dry thoroughly before beginning your project.

More small hearts. Avoid synthetic blends, which are forms of plastic and will melt quickly.

Vampire Sleep Shirt

(Uses pattern on page 139.)

Supplies:

- 100% cotton T-shirt
- Water soluble fabric pen
- Large sheet of cardboard
- Straight pins
- Variable-temperature burning unit
- Standard writing tip
- Spoon or medium square shader tip
- Fabric paint: red and white
- Spray bottle

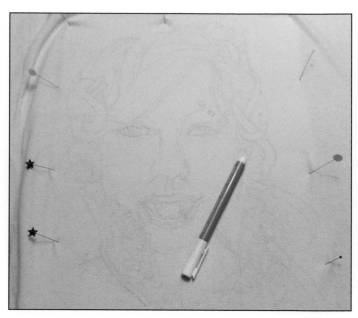

1 **Work surface.** Cut a large sheet of cardboard slightly smaller than the width of your T-shirt. Slide the cardboard inside the T-shirt. The cardboard will provide a stiff surface to stretch and pin the fabric and protect the back of the T-shirt from accidental burns. Make a copy of your pattern. Slide the pattern under the front of the T-shirt into position on your cardboard. Anchor the three layers together at the top edge of your pattern with several straight pins. On light-colored fabric you will be able to see the pattern lines through the fabric. Trace your outlines using a water-soluble fabric pen.

2 **Keep fabric smooth.** With your fingers, smooth the fabric to lie flat against the cardboard, slightly spreading the fabric. Use straight pins to secure the T-shirt to the cardboard. Make the fabric smooth and secure. Do not stretch it—stretching distorts the fabric's grain.

3 **Low temperature.** Begin burning at a low temperature. Using the standard writing tip, test the temperature setting by burning a few strands of hair. Slowly raise the temperature setting until you establish an even medium-tone burn line.

4 **Fine detailing.** Cloth takes fine detailing extremely well. This design was worked primarily with fine straight tightly packed lines for the hair, feathers, and ruffles. A small amount of shading was used in the eyelid areas, inside of the mouth, and along the right side of the face under the hair. Layering the lines on shading created the dark areas in this burn. Do not use a touch-and-lift stroke of fabric as this can burn through the fabric.

5 Water mist. After completing the burning, mist the entire T-shirt front with clean water to remove the water soluble fabric pen lines. Blot any excess water with a clean cloth. Allow the T-shirt to dry.

6 Detail and shade. The completed burn has dark eyes, lots of fine detailing, and a touch of shading to create this vampire's face.

7 Accents. Use fabric paint to add a few accents. For this project, use bright red on the lips and white for the eye highlights.

Wood

Pyrography is often called *woodburning* because wood is the most commonly used substratum. Wood provides a smooth, even working surface, a variety of basic color tones, and easy-to-use pre-manufactured shapes.

Basswood, birch, and poplar are the most popular wood species for pyrography, but as you grow in your craft you may wish to try maple, butternut, walnut, and mahogany.

The natural color of the wood affects the color ranges you will be able to see in your burning. Obviously the poplar, birch and basswood—all white woods—are going to show a range of pale value burns. African mahogany and the black walnut probably will not show the burning until you reach a mid or dark tone.

Pre-manufactured shapes such as wooden boxes, plaques, or canisters can be purchased at larger craft stores and supply houses. As your skill in woodburning grows, you may also consider using unfinished furniture as a work surface.

Whichever wood surfaces you chose, please consider basic safety procedures. Do not burn any painted, sealed, or oiled surface. Safe woodburning is done on untreated, raw wood only.

Soft woods, such as basswood and poplar, develop dark tones at low temperatures. You do need to watch your temperature settings so you do not go too quickly to very dark tones. Mahogany tends to burn at a medium-temperature range, while birch and black walnut need hotter temps.

Plywood. All of these samples are plywood—either three-ply or core center: birch, poplar, basswood, mahogany, and black walnut. All burn beautifully.

The grain and texture of the wood you select for your pyrography project can play an important role in the look of the finished project.

Wood differences: two examples

Three common woods for pyrography are basswood, poplar, and mahogany; each has its own specific coloration that affects the tonal values of your finished design.

Christmas Lamb and Sheltie (below left), for instance, is worked on ¼" (6mm) thick mahogany plywood. The rich red tones and thick, obvious grain of the mahogany begin this burning in the mid-range tones. To compensate for the wood's coloring, the burning uses a large amount of unburned highlight areas and deeply burned dark tones.

Two texturing strokes were used for *Christmas Lamb and Sheltie*—the fine line and random doodle. A light accent of red colored pencil on the inner ribbon and white along the ribbon's edge completes the work.

The design for this men's jewelry box, *Griffin Eagle* (below right), was worked on a pre-manufactured craft box. In the photo, you can see that the box lid was created using two pieces of wood glued just below the centerline of the box lid.

As the pyrography developed, a tonal value distinction between the two wood pieces became evident with the lower piece burning to a slightly darker tonal value than the upper wood piece.

Many times the type of wood used to manufacture blank wooden craft boxes, serving trays, and shapes is not identified. As some woods can be toxic, work pre-made, unlabeled wood in a well-ventilated workspace. If you have any reactions during the burn, such as irritated eyes, congestion, or skin rashes, stop burning immediately. This is not a common event but is worthy to note.

Christmas Lamb and Sheltie—done on mahogany plywood. (Uses pattern on page 140.)

Griffin Eagle—using a pre-manufactured box. (Uses pattern on page 141.)

Bengal Tiger

(Uses pattern on page 142.)

Tonal or gray scale values refer to how dark or light a burned area appears in your work. The palest values in a woodburning are those not burned at all. Instead, the raw wood is used for the sepia tone of that area. The darkest tonal value will be areas you burn at high temperatures to a near black tone. A range of tones, from pale tans to mid-browns and on into dark browns, falls between the two extremes.

This range of tonal values, worked from the palest progressively through the mid-tones into the black, is called a tonal value scale. Tonal value scales are called gray scales when you are working with black-and-white photographs. For woodburnings, they are called sepia value scales because of the soft beige through rich deep browns of the burned wood.

In woodburning, how pale or dark your tonal value for an area becomes depends on the temperature setting of your burning unit, the time the tip touches the wood, and how loosely or tightly packed your burn strokes are in an area.

The tiger portrait is divided into five tonal values:

- **black** for around the eyes, nose and mouth
- **dark** for the wide facial stripes
- **medium** for the shading along the sides of his face, chin, and nose
- **pale** for light shading through the nose, forehead, and under the eyes
- **white** (unburned) areas in what would be the white stripes of his face.

Bengal Tiger. A study in tonal value scales on wood.

Supplies:

- 8" x 8" (20cm x 20cm) birch plywood
- variable-temperature burning unit
- standard writing tip
- matte acrylic spray sealer

Sepia Value Scale for Bengal Tiger

1 **Dark tonal value.** After tracing the pattern to the wood, I worked my dark tonal values using a medium-high temperature setting. For my unit, that is a setting between 6 and 6.5 on my dial. I have used a tightly packed short line stroke that was worked with the direction of the wood grain. As I worked, I moved the tool tip in a slow smooth motion across the wood. The slow motion, tightly packed strokes, and medium-high setting gave me an even deep brown tonal value.

Scrubbie stroke. The scrubbie stroke is made with a quick back and forth motion. The number of small scrubbie lines and the number of layers of burning determine the tonal value.

Short strokes. Because the scrubbie stroke uses very short lines, there is a large amount of overlapping in any one layer of work. The overlap creates small dark spots and extra dark lines—perfect for a tiger's fur. Working the stroke with the grain of the birch plywood adds to the fur effect.

2 Medium tonal value. To lighten the tonal value in the next areas to be burned, I turned down my temperature setting to just below 6, a medium setting for my unit. Otherwise, I have used the same slow movement with the grain to burn the tightly packed short line strokes. The simple adjustment to my temperature setting has created a new tonal value of medium brown.

3 Pale tonal value. For my pale value burned areas, I turned down my temperature setting to about 5.5, a low-medium setting for my unit. I have increased the speed of my burning motion. This keeps the tool tip on the wood for a minimal amount of time. I have also allowed more space between each short line stroke. This small amount of space allows some of the raw wood to show through the burned area, helping to keep this area in a pale tan tonal value.

4 Black tonal value. My black tones were worked last by turning my temperature back to 6.5 and by using a very slow motion with the tool tip. Again I used a tightly packed short line stroke to fill the areas around the eyes, nostrils, and mouth. I now have a completed burning with little or no texture and no outlining or detailing. The entire pattern was worked only by using four burned tonal values and the white of the raw, unburned wood. With tonal value alone I have created a Bengal tiger's face. The completed project has distinct tonal values from the white of the wood through the black tones surrounding the eyes.

Steampunk Dragonfly

(Uses pattern on page 138.)

Gears and pulleys, electrical wire connectors and pressure gauges, vintage rhinestone beads, and antique brass filigree combine to renew that wonderful turn-of-the-century feeling in the Steampunk art style now becoming part of the American pop culture mainstream.

The *Dragonfly Steam Punk Gear* project features a filigree winged dragonfly with a nuts, bolts, and threaded pipe body. The dragonfly rests on acanthus leaf-decorated flexible electrical conduit and the tail turns into a coiled loop. Behind the dragonfly rest six steel gears held together by two leaf screw plates, four more coil loops, an electrical gauge with a wing nut, and one latch hook. To add to the whimsical feeling, watercolor pencils were used to complete the design with bright, easy to apply colors.

Project notes

Each pyrography system uses a slightly different temperature for the number settings on the dial. Each wood species burns to a medium sepia tone at a different temperature. Do a test sample burning using the same species of wood to determine your exact temperature settings before you begin working on your project board.

For my practice board, worked on poplar plywood, I used the following settings:

- 3½ for **pale** value tones

- 4 for **mid-tone sepia brown** value tones

- 4½ for **strong, dark mid-tone sepia** value

- 5 for **black** tones

- 6 caused **scorching or haloing** along the burn lines

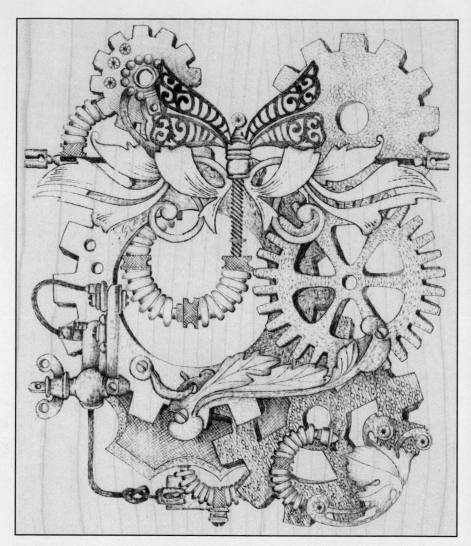

Related elements. Many pyrography patterns are simple line art without shading or a gray scale drawing that could be used to determine our burning strokes or shading placement. This project guides you through the process of shading a line art design. The project teaches how to group related elements, use repetitive textures to unite elements in the pattern, and how to determine where your shadows fall.

Starting

Generally, I start woodburning projects using very pale tonal values to establish each elemental area. As the burning progresses through the steps, I rework any area to a darker tonal value if it is needed. Start any pyrography project with pale light strokes and add more layers as needed to create depth.

This project uses the standard writing tip for the fine line and texture strokes. A few textures in the gears and electrical connectors use a spoon shader tip pen. These two burning tips work best for me. Take time to practice with the pen tips you have available to determine which tip creates the best results for you.

Note: I tend to move from one area of the pattern to another, one texturing stroke into a new texture, and from one aspect of pattern development into another. I will move from working the organic leaves to working some hard metal areas, from establishing the pale and dark tone values, and then move into creating the depth perspective on the gears.

Many pyrographers will completely work and finish one element of a design and then move onto a new element, creating the project one element at a time. I prefer to work a little on each element, slowly developing all areas of the pattern through progressive steps. This allows me to make changes to any area of the design at any time—strengthening a shadow, adding a few details, emphasizing a specific element, and adding or repeating textures.

Preparing the wood surface:

- I used poplar plywood. Also consider using basswood or birch as your substratum.

- Prepare your wood by carefully sanding the working surface with 320-grit sandpaper. Remove any dust using a tack cloth.

- Center a printed copy of the pattern on the board and tape the pattern in place using two or three pieces of transparent tape along one side of the paper. Slide a sheet of graphite tracing paper between the pattern paper and board with the graphite side against the wood. Use an ink pen or #2 pencil to trace along the pattern lines. Check that you have traced all of the pattern lines before you remove the pattern paper from the wood.

1 Following the contour. Using a temperature setting of 3½ for a pale tonal value coloring and my standard writing tip pen, I have shaded the acanthus leaves using a fine long line texture that follows the contour of the leaves. The shading for these leaves starts at the leaf tip and pulls into the center area of the leaf. A second area of shading is created where one area of the leaf or stem is tucked under another element. By working all of the leaf elements in the same manner at the same time they become united.

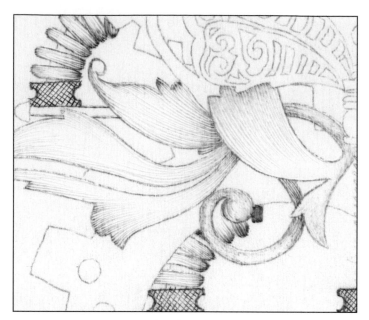

2 **Burning the conduit.** Work the electrical conduit areas next using the same fine long line stroke and a temperature setting of 3½. To give the appearance of a tight turn in the conduit loop, work the inside edge of each conduit section twice to darken it, leaving the outer edge of each coil section with only one layer of burning. The connecting nut in the center of each conduit loop has been worked in a crosshatch pattern. Changing the line texture of the burning from simple lines in the conduit to crosshatch in the connecting nuts separates the two design areas.

3 **Tonal range.** Creating a few extremely dark areas to contrast with the palest tones establishes the project's tonal value range. Work all other elements in the design in some tonal value between the two values. To pull the darkest tone into some other area of the design I also have worked the electrical cords in tight scrubbie strokes at the temperature setting of 5. I can add more pale tone areas and black tone elements as the burning develops. This step establishes the two endpoints of my tonal scale—the palest coloring and the darkest coloring .

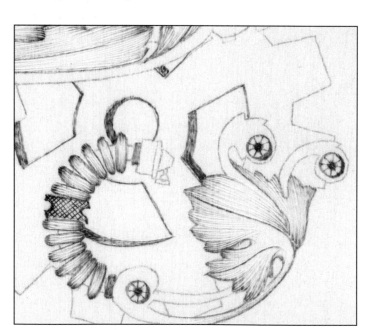

4 **Repetitive elements.** At this point, I have established my repetitive elements and my pale and black tonal range. Next, I need to determine where my depth perspective for the pattern will fall. The gears shown in the pattern are flat two-dimensional gears. For my burning, I want three dimensions to give an impression of thickness to the metal. I have worked a medium-sepia value using a temperature setting of 4 to create an inside edge to the openings and holes of the gears. All of these areas fall on the left or lower left of the gear outline. That inside edge adds the third dimension of thickness to the gears.

5 **Adding more depth.** Step 4 established the depth perspective for the gears. During this stage of the burning, I have carried that depth perspective to the outer-toothed edges of the gear. As with the inside holes, all of the shading falls on the left or lower left side of the teeth. The sides of the gear teeth have been worked at a temperature setting of 4½ to take them to a medium-dark tone.

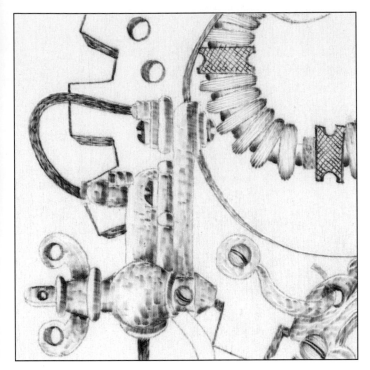

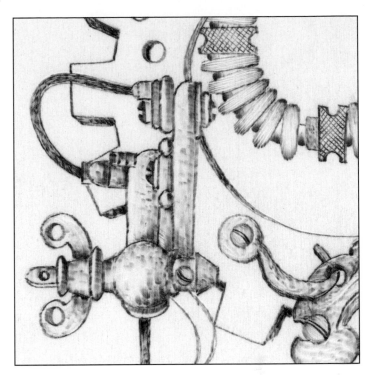

6 **Unique elements.** I am ready to move to some of my unique elements. I have used fine long contour lines for the leaf elements, long lines for the coiled loops, crosshatching for the coil loop connectors, and a tight scrubbie stroke for the dark values in the electric cord and gear side shadings. Using my spoon shader tip pen at a temperature setting of 4 to 4½, I used a simple touch-and-lift stroke. This creates a large spotted texture for this element. A second layer of touch-and-lift burning was done on the lower areas of the junction box where one area of the pattern touched or tucked under another.

7 **Outlining.** Returning to my standard writing tip pen and a medium temperature setting of 4, I have begun outlining some areas of my elements. By outlining this fun, whimsical pattern I can leave some areas of the pattern unburned as highlight areas. If this were a realistic design, I would outline only those areas that seemed weak or non-existent. By working this outlining step at a medium temperature I can always return to any area with a darker outline to strengthen that element, giving it more emphasis.

8 **Gear faces.** It is time to begin working on the gear faces. Using my standard writing tip and a temperature setting of 4½, I have worked the bottom left gear using a tight crosshatch stroke. I worked a second layer of crosshatching where the gear tucks under the two gears above it. The border area of the gear was worked using a touch-and-lift small spot stroke to create a new texture and establish that border as an independent area from the gear face.

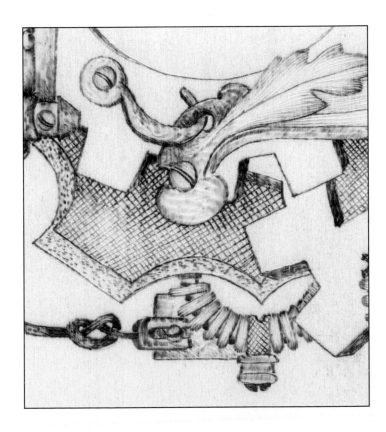

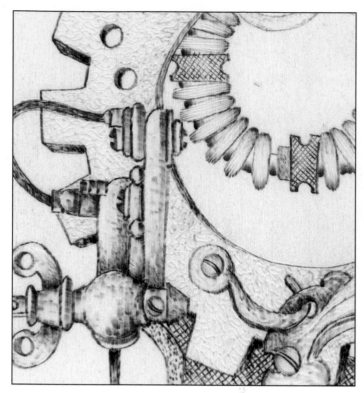

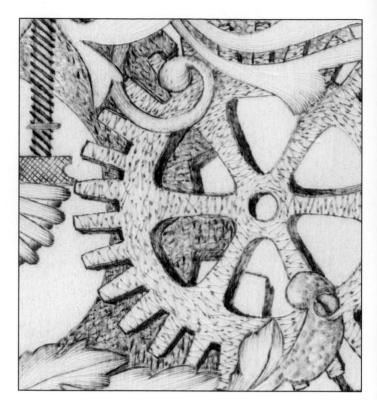

9 **Tiny circles.** Using a temperature setting between 3 and 4 and my standard writing tip, I burned tiny circles into the upper-right gear. The circles are tightly packed and fill the entire gear face surface. Where the upper-right gear tucks under the organic leaves and electric wire, a second layer of burning darkens the circle texture. Work the upper-left gear in fine straight lines with a crosshatch pattern where it tucks under the filigree wings of the dragonfly. Work the large central gear in a random doodle stroke. Place your pen tip onto the gear face and begin wandering in small loops and turn backs.

10 **Quick dash lines.** The center-right gear was worked at a temperature setting of 4. Using the side of my standard writing tip in a touch-and-lift stroke, I made small quick dash lines. These lines were laid down generally following the circular feeling of the gear, with some lines allowed to cross others.

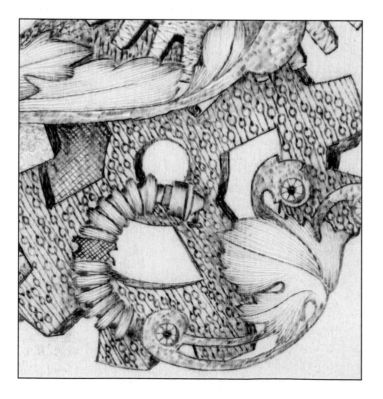

11 **Open circles.** For my last gear, lower right corner, I used a line stroke with small open circles. Pull a small section of the line, add a small open circle, return to the line stroke, and then add one or two more circles. Using my spoon shader tip pen and a temperature setting between 3 and 4, I laid down a light layer of shading to some areas in the gear using a gentle touch-and-pull stroke that creates an even coloring of sepia over the area. Adding this layer of shading darkens both the area and the texture strokes already been burned into an area.

12 **Nearing completion.** The burning for this project is nearly complete. At this point, I have set my plaque up on my table and stepped back from the work for a while. Take time to look over your work to discover what areas are strong and bold compared to areas that might need strengthening with a darker outline. I also check my shading to see where a slightly darker tonal value might be needed to push the element deeper into the background. I darkened many of the perspective areas on the gear holes and teeth into my black tonal value. I added more black tones to the overall design and emphasized the gear teeth. I added a layer of shading to the largest middle gear to the bottom background gear to push these two elements behind the upper gears. A few areas of black outline accents were added throughout the design, particularly in the leaf elements and the dragonfly's body.

13 **Completed.** Burning for this project is now complete. Take time to use a white artist eraser to remove any remaining tracing lines from your plaque. Dust the plaque well to remove any eraser fibers. You can stop at this point, leaving the project in the wood burning stage. If you do not want to add color, apply several coats of polyurethane or acrylic gloss spray sealer or paste wax to seal the project.

Steampunk Dragonfly: Quick Review

- **Look for repeated elements that can all be worked in the same manner at the same time.** For the Steampunk Dragonfly, there are six repeated elements.

- **Use the same texturing stroke or the same tonal value coloring to unite similar elements.** The organic leaf elements were worked in long line strokes in a pale tonal value.

- **To separate similar elements use a different texture stroke for each element.** Each of the six gears has its own, unique texture.

- **Determine where you need to add perspective depth in the pattern and work that depth burning on all the elements at one time.** The open holes of the gears and the gear teeth were worked on the same side of the gears at the same tonal value.

- **A pale or medium tonal value outlining will allow you to use unburned areas in the design for highlights.** The electrical junction box uses unburned highlights surrounded by a light or pale tonal value outlining.

- **Add a second layer of burning work where you want your shadows to fall.** Adding layers of burning deepens the tonal value of the area. For many fun designs, shading falls on the background element where it tucks under or goes behind another element.

- **Use dark tonal value accent outlining in just a few areas of your pattern.** Use it only to strengthen an area that seems undefined or needs extra emphasis.

- **Develop your burning slowly beginning with pale tones.** You can always add more shading or darken an elements tonal value as needed and as more of the design is worked.

Adding color

Adding color using a transparent coloring agent such as watercolors, watercolor pencils, or oil paint glazes does not change or alter how you do your woodburning strokes in any manner. However, adding color can diminish the impact of your woodburning strokes. To the eye, color is stronger and more important than shading. Balance your coloring work with your burning tonal values using darker colors over dark tonal value areas and pale colors on pale tones.

When using colored pencils, either wax-based or watercolor, keep your pencil extremely sharp. Use a gentle, light pressure to apply the color over the burned area. This keeps the coloring on the high unburned areas, within the element. Develop the coloring slowly by applying layers of pencil work.

Apply watercolor pencils dry from the pencil point and then blend them with a slightly damp soft bristle brush. Use several different colors in one area to add more interest to the coloring. When the pencil has been washed with the damp brush, the coloring in that area will deepen, so work in light layers of coloring at a time. New layers of pencil can be added, then washed, to give an area more color.

In our project, I have used three to four colors in many elements. The upper-left gear shown in the photo is worked using medium blue, medium purple, and sienna brown. The large gear below it has medium blue, medium teal, dark green, and yellow. These multiple colors are applied in a random manner.

Allow the completed project to thoroughly dry. Use several coats of polyurethane or acrylic spray sealer to add the finishing coat to your burning

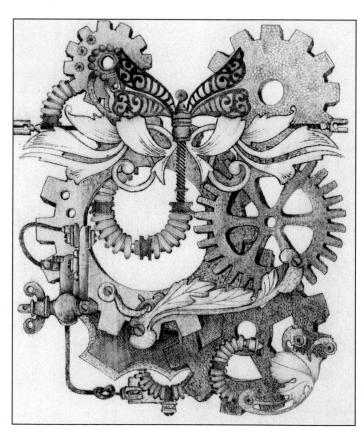

1 **Why artist-quality?** Colored pencils are wonderful for adding coloring to pyrography projects worked on wood, paper, or gourds. I personally prefer artist-quality watercolor pencils. These pencils contain little or no clay or wax base so they create clear transparent coloring. A set of twelve or twenty-four pencils is well worth the investment for any pyrographer.

2 **Using water.** Dampen a soft bristle brush with clean water. Wash a coating of water over the watercolor pencil working one element at a time. The more water you carry in your brush, the more the pencil colors will blend. Allow each element to dry before working an adjacent element with the damp brush. This will help limit the chance of the color from one element bleeding into an adjacent area.

PART FOUR

Project Patterns

Olson's Dairy Truck Pattern

Horse's Head Practice Board Pattern

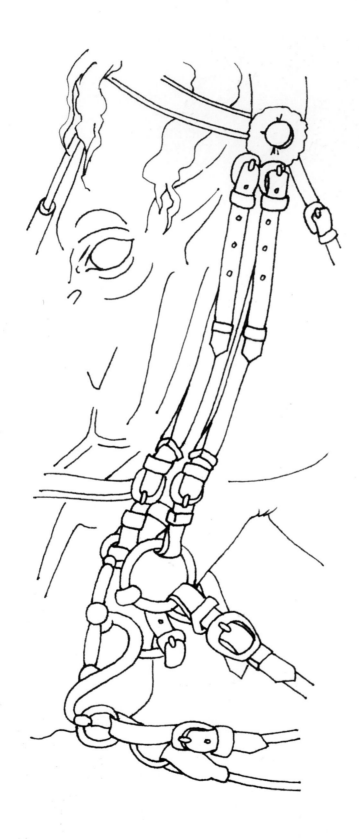

Civil War Generals Pattern

Blue Jay Mill Pattern

Totem Pole Pattern 1

Southwest Birdhouse Gourd Practice Board Patterns

Overlap point

A

B

Overlap point

Overlap point

A

B

Overlap point

Posies Cache Pot Pattern

Floral Birdhouse Pattern

Native American Bead Rattle Patterns

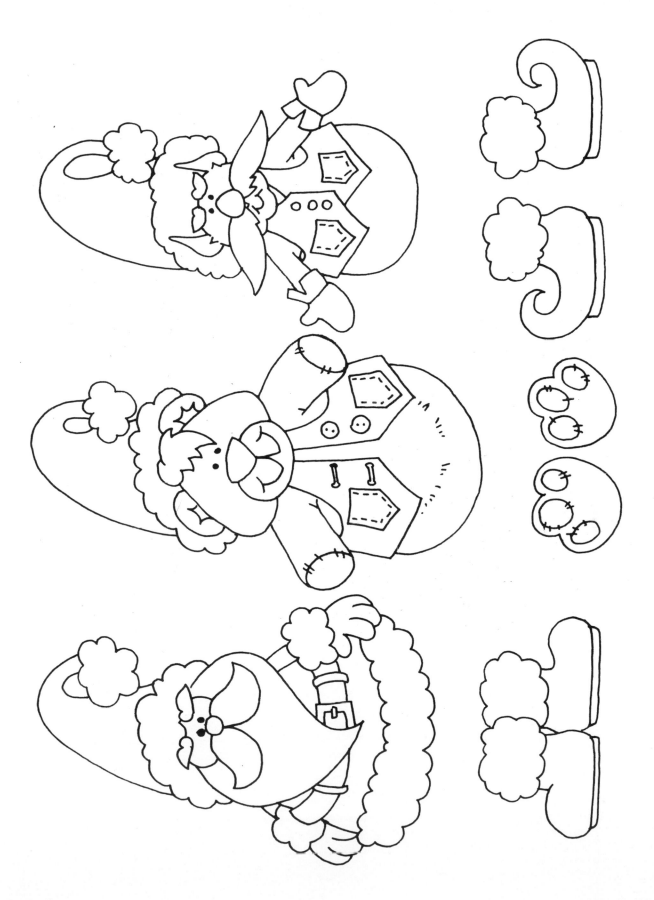

Steampunk Photo Frame Pattern

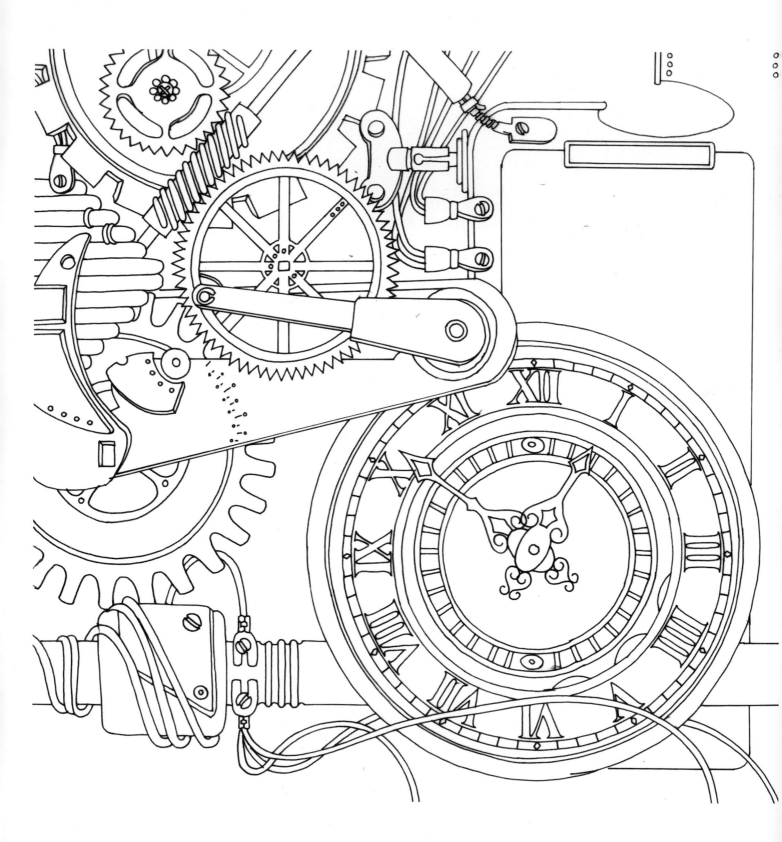

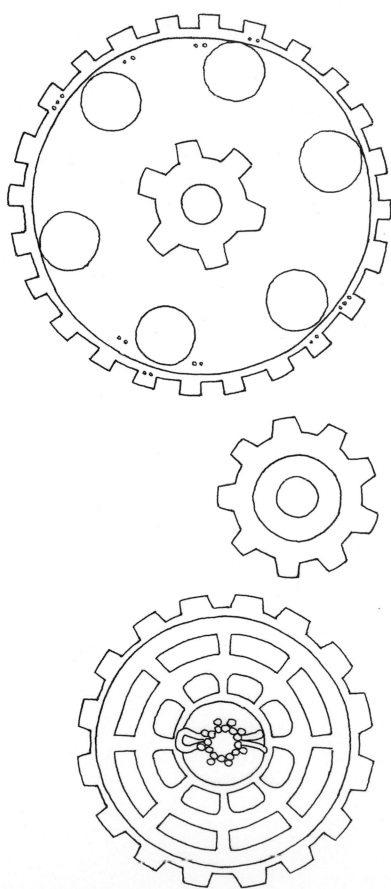

Daylily Cork Board Pattern

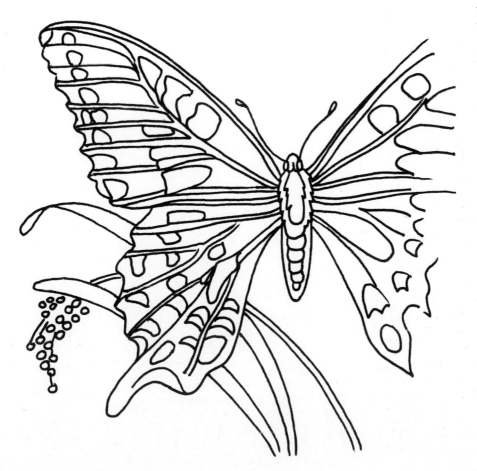

Peas Pattern

Pumpkin Pattern

Steampunk Dragonfly Pattern

Christmas Lamb and Sheltie Pattern

Bengal Tiger Pattern

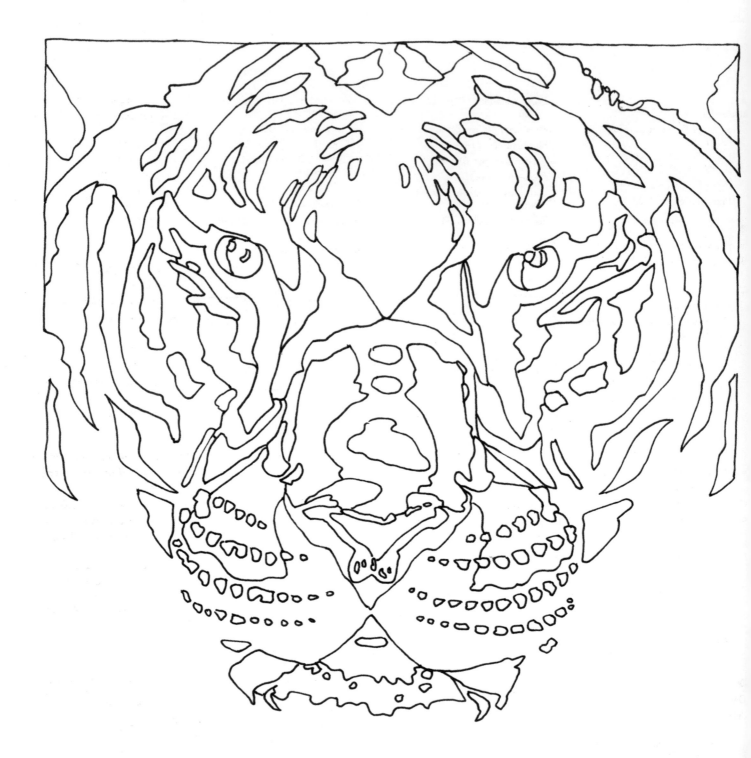

Index

Note: Page numbers in **bold** indicate projects. Page numbers in italics indicate patterns.

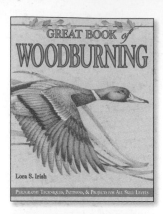
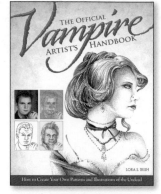
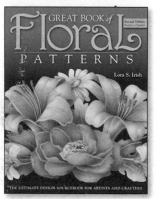
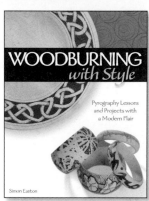
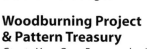